SERIAL

An Introduction to the Music of

COMPOSITION

Schoenberg, Berg, and Webern

AND

by George Perle

ATONALITY

FIFTH EDITION, REVISED

UNIVERSITY OF CALIFORNIA PRESS
Berkeley, Los Angeles, London • 1981

In Memory of My Mother

University of California Press,
Berkeley and Los Angeles, California
University of California Press, Limited
London, England
©1962, 1980 by The Regents of the University of California
Second Edition, 1968
Third Edition, 1972
Fourth Edition, 1977
Fifth Edition, 1981
ISBN: 0-520-04365-0
Library of Congress Catalog Card Number 80-53772
Manufactured in the United States of America

1 2 3 4 5 6 7 8 9

Contents

Preface
TO THE FIFTH EDITION

Serial Composition and Atonality, in this new edition, is still what it has always been: an introduction to the technical features of a body of work that probably represents the most far-reaching and thoroughgoing revolution the history of music has known since the beginnings of polyphony. In the analysis of specific compositions there is first and last of all a concern with the musical surface — an attempt to trace connections and distinctions *there* before offering any deeper-level constructions, and to offer none where their efforts are not obvious on more immediate levels of musical experience.

If, however, my original purpose and method have not changed, if this book remains what its sub-title asserts it to be, *An Introduction to the Music of Schoenberg, Berg, and Webern,* this does not imply that my views respecting this music have not evolved in the past twenty years. Insights that are the products of that evolution are summarized in the final chapter of my recent book, *Twelve-Tone Tonality,* where a composition that is discussed in detail in the following pages is briefly mentioned as giving a fundamental role to a four-note collection ("cell y" in ex. 15, below) whose structural functions in the movement can be summarized in the following examples:

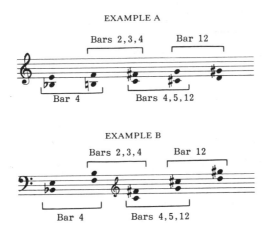

Such a reduction reveals inherent properties of the cell and a structural background shared with other works whose surface features may unfold totally different "styles" of composition. The importance of the fact that such common background structures can sometimes be demonstrated in post-tonal music is self-evident. But one should not *begin* with such generalized constructions in the initial stages of analyzing the music with which we are here concerned, nor assume their necessary presence.

In this instance an intermediate level of analysis, linking the description of surface relations on pages 16–18 below with the ultimate reduction illustrated above, is possible. The overall unfolding of the two basic cells through "overlapping common elements" as described in the first, third, and sixth paragraphs of the analysis on pp. 16–18 may be summarized in either of the following diagrams, the first showing the progression as moving through two segments of the cycle of semitones, the second as moving through two segments of the cycle of fifths:[1]

EXAMPLE C

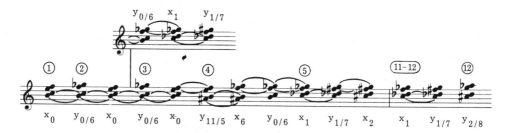

EXAMPLE D

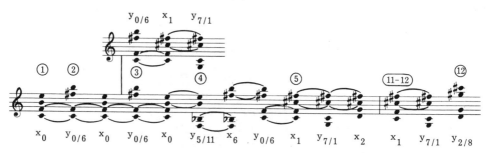

Examples C and D demonstrate the special meaning of cell x as a bridge between the various transpositions of cell y. If, to borrow the terminology employed by Schenker to distinguish hierarchical levels in tonal composition, the discussion on pages 16–18 is primarily concerned with the foreground and examples A and B exclusively concerned with the background, examples C and D may be described as middleground sketches. They significantly deepen our understanding of the movement and I had considered incorporating them in the body of the text of this new edition and of making a few comparable additions elsewhere. But then new problems of presentation and analysis arose.

---

[1]Subscripts to "x" and "y" show their pitch level relative to x_0 and y_0. The two integers for "y" indicate that tritone transpositions are equivalent as to pitch-class content.

What is the relation of the x–y progression represented in examples C and D to the seven-note figure in bars 6, 10, and 12–13 and to the contrasting middle section of the movement, bars 7–10? Here one is on more speculative ground and must be ready to accept ambiguities. And were I to add the intermediate level of explanation illustrated in examples C and D, would I not also wish to show what it is intermediate to and include examples A and B as well? And then one will want to go on to show how and why the structural functions of the cell illustrated in examples A and B are inherent, and their compositional implications for Bartók's *Fourth Quartet*, Berg's *Lulu*, Webern's *Symphony*, etc. (as, in fact, I do in *Twelve-Tone Tonality*). Where does one stop? There is nothing analogous to a four-note cell with inherent structural functions to suggest a closed design for a book like this.

In the first paragraph of Chapter II, I suggest that "an unprecedented degree of ambiguity attaches to the individual progression in general" in "free" atonality, since the " 'rightness' of a particular note depends not upon its possible containment within a preestablished harmonic unit, as it does in tonality, but upon larger compositional factors whose meaning must be discovered within the work itself." But the preceding examples have just demonstrated that to some degree we can in fact speak of "preestablished harmonic units" in respect to Webern's Opus 5, No. 4. The "augmented triad" functions as such a "preestablished harmonic unit" in Schoenberg's Opus 11, No. 1.[2] The context in which it does so is much more complex and problematical, but it seems clear that the overall structure is largely determined by the properties of the interval-4 cycle and its partitioning of the semitonal scale into four discrete segments. This view of the movement was already offered in the first edition of this book, before my attention had been called to the notational discrepancy in bar 55 (see note 4, p. 15, below) which appears in all editions that preceded the publication of this piece in the *Gesamtausgabe* in 1968, and when I was still, like everyone else, reading *c*♯ rather than *b*♯ in the right-hand part, second beat. A consequence of this latter reading is that all four "augmented triads" appear in sequence in this and the following bar, to confirm and clarify, at a strategic moment in the formal design, the harmonic basis of the composition. This is another and even stronger argument for resolving the notational discrepancy in favor of *b*♯, to add to the excellent ones offered by Edward T. Cone in taking issue with the "correction" given in the *Gesamtausgabe:* "Misguidedly, I had looked forward in the present publication to a confirmation of *b*♯, which creates an augmented triad that sounds to me much more idiomatic here than the minor triad formed by the apparently correct *c*♯; even the major-minor clash produced by the latter seems insufficiently dissonant, within the vocabulary of this piece, to support the crescendo that it must. Hence I am inclined to mistrust the accepted solution, even if it turns out to have the authority of the manuscript behind it. The misprint might have arisen as a result of a

---

[2] Cf. the discussion of "reflexive" and "non-reflexive" elements in the concluding chapter of *Twelve-Tone Tonality*.

correction or a revision made by the engraver or the printer."[3] The *Kritischer Bericht* for this volume of the *Gesamtausgabe* has since been published (1975), and it does, in fact, "have the authority of the manuscript" for the solution that it offers. Schoenberg's first draft has the $c\sharp$ and so does a copy in another hand, presumably made from Schoenberg's missing fair copy, which may have been the basis for the first edition. In the present instance contextual considerations ought surely to play a role in weighing the evidence for one or another solution to the textual discrepancy, just as they do in the examples from Mozart, Chopin, and Beethoven cited by Mr. Cone in his article. The musical evidence still inclines me "to mistrust the accepted solution." This may be a "mistake" of the type cited by Mr. Cone, one that "may have crept in between the manuscript and the printed edition."[4] Elsewhere I have argued against a "fundamental error" in the analysis of much of this music: "the failure to make a qualitative distinction between a musical system, diatonic tonality, in which every harmony is referable to a single type of chord structure, and musical systems (or nonsystems) in which there is no such *a priori* referential harmonic structure;"[5] to ignore all considerations of contextual logic and coherence in making judgments about this music seems to me a "fundamental error" of the opposite nature but of similar magnitude.

The concluding remarks to the collaborative essays on "Twelve-Note Composition" and "Atonality" by Paul Lanksy and myself in the sixth edition of *Grove's Dictionary* may be appropriately repeated here:

"Perhaps the most important influence of Schoenberg's method is not the 12-note idea in itself, but along with it the individual concepts of permutation, inversional symmetry and complementation, invariance under transformation, aggregate construction, closed systems, properties of adjacency as compositional determinants, transformations of musical surfaces through predefined operations, and so on. Each of these ideas by itself, or in conjunction with many others, is focused upon with varying degrees of sharpness in the music of such different composers as Bartók, Stravinsky, Schoenberg, Berg, Webern, Varèse, etc. In this sense the development of the serial idea may be viewed not as a radical break with the past but as an especially brilliant coordination of musical ideas which had developed in the course of recent history. The symmetrical divisions of the octave so often found in Liszt and Wagner, for example, are not momentary aberrations in tonal music which led to its ultimate destruction, but, rather, important musical ideas which, in defying integration into a given concept of a musical language challenged the boundaries of that language."

---

[3] "Editorial Responsibility and Schoenberg's Troublesome 'Misprints,'" *Perspectives of New Music*, XI/1 (1972), pp. 70 ff.

[4] Ibid., p. 75.

[5] Perle, review of *Studien zur Entwicklung des dodekaphonen Satzes bei Arnold Schönberg*, by Jan Maegaard, *Musical Quarterly*, LXIII (1977), p. 278.

"The tendency of historical criticism to construct systems of classification which attempt to index individual entries as neatly and unambiguously as possible has certainly been frustrated so far by musical thought in the 20th century. The highly individual and unique nature of the contributions of Schoenberg, Bartók, Webern, Berg, and others, ultimately transcends and trivializes such attempts, if it does not contradict them."

G.P., 1980

Preface

TO THE FIRST EDITION

The single most impressive musical development since World War II has been the astonishingly rapid and widespread dissemination of the practice of twelve-tone composition. In the very recent past the twelve-tone movement was regarded as the concern only of a few sectarians. Today it is no novelty to find the modern jazz artist improvising on a tone row, the young music student writing a twelve-tone piece for his composition class, the choreographer converting a twelve-tone classic into ballet music. It is only in the most backward circles that the mere use of a tone row will secure a composer's position as a member of the avant-garde, as it was sure to do only a few years ago.

Unfortunately, there is little evidence in the theoretical writings on atonality and the twelve-tone system to show that this development is paralleled by a comparable growth in understanding of the technical features of the music of Arnold Schoenberg, Alban Berg, and Anton Webern, the founders of the movement. One group of enthusiastic polemicists for this music specializes in "analyses" that rarely consist of anything more than tabulations of the notes of the set in their ramified course throughout the composition, on the assumption that the mere identification of the order numbers of the notes will establish their validity. Another group claims to speak for a new avant-garde, in an official publication behind whose formidable diagrams, graphs, and mathematical formulas there lurks a naïve and all-pervasive mysticism, summed up by one composer in the concluding words of his description of one of his "totally organized" works: "The paradox of ultimate necessity's causing unpredictable chance." This group, like the other, establishes "ultimate necessity" by labeling the notes with their appropriate order numbers, the only distinction being the added "complexity" that results from the serialization not only of pitches but also of dynamics, rhythm, and other "parameters," and from plotting the elements not only in their original serial order from 1 to 12 but also in various rotations and permutations of the original ordering. As I have pointed out in a recent article, this type of "analysis" is as meaningless as would be "the labeling of the notes of a tonal composition to indicate their scale-degrees."[1]

---

[1]George Perle, "Theory and Practice in Twelve-Tone Music," *The Score*, 1959, 58 ff. This article was a contribution to a discussion initiated by Peter Stadlen in his article, "Serialism Reconsidered," *The Score*, February 1958, 12 ff.

The "free" atonality that preceded the twelve-tone system is even less adequately dealt with in the literature, much of which either ignores this music entirely or else limits itself to the description of isolated details whose connection with the whole is never explained except in terms of farfetched motivic associations. Relying on these descriptions alone, the reader might justifiably assume that the musical details are transferable at will from one composition to another, since the only observations that relate to the total work are a few generalizations, employing, without definition, such terms as "nonrepetition" and "perpetual variation." This confusion concerning the technical character of the music is finally confounded by explanations in terms of historical and aesthetic motivations.

My main purpose in the present study is to offer a comprehensive description and a critical examination of the technical procedures employed in the atonal and twelve-tone compositions of Schoenberg, Berg, and Webern. It has seemed important to stress that the concept of a "series" or "set" is not unique to "Schoenberg and his School." There is some discussion, therefore, of nondodecaphonic serial procedures as employed in selected works by Debussy, Scriabin, Roslavetz, Bartók, and Stravinsky.

As the table of contents indicates, the subject matter is developed systematically rather than chronologically. Sufficient data are provided, however, to permit the reader to reconstruct an approximate chronology. Where there is a significant discrepancy between dates of composition and publication of a work, both dates are given. However, several important works are not mentioned and others are discussed only very briefly, since this book does not aim at either biographical or bibliographical completeness.

I wish to express my gratitude to Dr. Gustave Reese, who was kind enough to read the original manuscript with great care and to assist me in clarifying a number of obscure formulations. Most of the concepts presented I discussed at length with the young American composer Richard Swift long before their appearance here. Mr. Swift also gave generously of his time and energy in the reading and criticism, prior to publication, not only of this book but also of many of my earlier writings, and I am glad of this opportunity to express my appreciation. Certain aspects—perhaps the most significant—of the work of Schoenberg and Webern have been elucidated for the first time by Milton Babbitt, who has also been the first to provide twelve-tone theory with a consistent technical vocabulary. For this reason frequent references are made in this volume to Mr. Babbitt's contributions.

The reader's attention is called to a recent publication of the University of California Press, *Serial Music: A Classified Bibliography of Writings on Twelve-Tone and Electronic Music,* by Ann Phillips Basart.

If, as a result of my efforts, the composition of twelve-tone music shall have become more difficult, I shall feel amply rewarded.

G.P., 1962

I

Tonality, Atonality, Dodecaphony

Atonality originates in an attempt to liberate the twelve notes of the chromatic scale from the diatonic functional associations they still retain in "chromatic" music—to dissociate, so to speak, the chromatic scale from "chromaticism." The expanded harmonic vocabulary of late nineteenth-century music had extended the range of tonal relationships to the point where the traditional articulative procedures were no longer adequate. The final step in this development was taken by Arnold Schoenberg in a radical stylistic departure based upon a rejection of any general principles regulating simultaneity and progression. In the compositions Schoenberg wrote between 1908 and 1923, the period of "free" atonality, he disclosed that this ultimate expansion of possible relations to include the whole range of combinations contained in the semitonal scale demands a revaluation of every aspect of the musical language.

The composer working within the diatonic tonal system may take for granted the existence of specific properties of that system: a seven-tone scale, triadic harmonic structure, a key center, and so forth. The atonal composer, however, can take for granted nothing except the existence of a given limiting sound world, the semitonal scale. Aside from this assumption, it is impossible to state the fundamental conditions of atonality *in general*, except in a negative way, merely stipulating the absence of a priori functional connections among the twelve notes of the semitonal scale. Musical coherence requires additional limiting factors, but these are not reducible to a set of foundational assumptions in terms of which the compositions that are collectively designated by the expression "atonal music" can be said to represent a "system" of composition.

In 1923 Schoenberg first published a composition employing the "method of composing with twelve notes." This "method" soon proved to have some general relevance to the special problems of atonal composition. It is consistent with both the positive and negative premises of atonality, affirming the availability of twelve notes while denying a priori functional precedence to any one of them.

1

In Schoenberg's twelve-tone system all the tone relations that govern a given musical context are referable to a specific linear ordering of the twelve notes of the semitonal scale. Neither register, duration, timbre, or intensity—in other words, no attribute other than that represented by the pitch-class name of what is informally called a "note"[1]—is defined by this referential permutation of the semitonal scale, a permutation denoted by the term "row," "series," or "set."[2] An unambiguous ordering is assumed; but the degree to which this ordering actually determines the general musical procedures varies greatly from one work to another, even where these are by the same composer. The total musical texture inevitably entails intervallic relations not directly specified by the set, and even on a purely linear plane deviations occur. Yet the premise of an ordered arrangement of the twelve notes, if it is to have any meaning, must somehow govern the essential musical events in a consistent and logical manner, in spite of ambiguities and licenses. The possibility of modification, however momentary, of the preestablished order implies the occasional presence of further preconditions. What these are, and what their relation is to the essential preconditions, will be discussed in detail later.

The following postulates, then, must be understood to refer only to the set on which a given work, or section of a work,[3] may be based. The compositional implications of these postulates are the subject of Chapters IV, V, and VI of this book.

1. The set comprises all twelve notes of the semitonal scale, arranged in a specific linear order.

2. No note appears more than once within the set.

3. The set is statable in any of its linear aspects: prime, inversion, retrograde, and retrograde-inversion.

---

[1]Cf. Milton Babbitt, "Twelve-Tone Invariants as Compositional Determinants," *The Musical Quarterly,* XLVI (1960), 246 ff. This issue has been reprinted as *Problems of Modern Music* (New York: Norton, 1960).

[2]The accepted German term *Reihe* may mean "row," "series," or "set." Of these, "row," the earliest to gain acceptance in writings in English on the subject, is the least appropriate, since it implies a certain regularity, not necessarily characteristic of the set. To a large extent it was replaced by "series," mainly through the books and articles of Ernst Krenek. The term "set," introduced in 1946 by Milton Babbitt in *The Function of Set Structure in the Twelve-Tone System* (reproduced in typescript by Princeton University, Dept. of Music), has gained general currency.

[3]The reason that the extent of the musical area governed by a particular set is not specifically delimited here is given in Chap. IV, "Motivic Functions of the Set." A "rule" to the effect that a composition should be based on a single set is given in practically every presentation of the principles of Schoenberg's twelve-tone system (see Josef Rufer, *Composition with Twelve Notes* [New York: The Macmillan Co., 1954], pp. 106 ff., and Schoenberg's own statement, quoted therein: "It does not seem right to me to use more than one series"). Webern's works conform to this "rule," but it is not an adequate formulation of the practice of either Schoenberg or Berg. In the twelve-tone system devised by Josef Hauer (see below) there is free progression from one set, or "trope," to another.

4. The set in each of its four transformations (that is, linear aspects) is statable upon any degree of the semitonal scale.

In the examples, black unstemmed noteheads will stand for pitch-class names. The integers from 0 to 11 can be substituted for pitch-class names by assigning these integers to the successive notes of an ascending semitonal scale whose initial element, pitch-class no. 0, will be the same as the first note of a given prime form of the set. Thus, example 4 can be represented as

$$0 \quad 11 \quad 7 \quad 8 \quad 3 \quad 1 \quad 2 \quad 10 \quad 6 \quad 5 \quad 4 \quad 9$$

This form of the set is "P-0," that is, the prime set at what is assumed as "transposition no. 0." If this form is transposed to, say, the "perfect fifth" above, it will be identified as "P-7" and its numerical representation can be deduced by adding 7 to each pitch-class number of P-0. Where the resulting sum is 12 or more, 12 (representing the octave) should be subtracted. Thus, P-7 will read, in pitch-class number notation,

$$7 \quad 6 \quad 2 \quad 3 \quad 10 \quad 8 \quad 9 \quad 5 \quad 1 \quad 0 \quad 11 \quad 4$$

The numerical representation of the inversion at a given transposition number may be deduced by subtracting each pitch-class number of P-0 from that transposition number or from that transposition number plus 12. Thus, I-5 will read, in pitch-class number notation.

$$5 \quad 6 \quad 10 \quad 9 \quad 2 \quad 4 \quad 3 \quad 7 \quad 11 \quad 0 \quad 1 \quad 8$$

The interval succession of a set is the series of integers determined by subtracting each pitch-class number from the following or from the latter plus 12. Thus, the prime form of the set, regardless of transposition, will be represented by the following series of interval numbers:

$$11 \quad 8 \quad 1 \quad 7 \quad 10 \quad 1 \quad 8 \quad 8 \quad 11 \quad 11 \quad 5$$

The complementary interval numbers (the differences when each interval number of the prime set is subtracted from 12) will represent the inversion:

$$1 \quad 4 \quad 11 \quad 5 \quad 2 \quad 11 \quad 4 \quad 4 \quad 1 \quad 1 \quad 7$$

Whereas the retrograde of a given set may be found by reading the pitch-class number succession of its prime form backwards, the same procedure applied to the interval number succession of the prime will give the interval number succession of the retrograde-inversion. Similarly, the pitch-class number succession of the inversion read backwards gives the pitch-class number succession of the retrograde-inversion, while the interval number succession of the inversion read backwards gives the interval number succession of the retrograde.[4]

The term "set-complex" refers to the forty-eight different forms generated when a given series is stated at all twelve transpositions in each of its four aspects. The term "set-form" refers to any given member of this complex. It is immaterial which aspect of a given set is designated as the prime, so long as the

---

[4]See Babbitt, n. 1, above.

remaining terms are properly interchanged in order to reflect the reciprocal relations among the set-forms.[5] (In twelve-tone music there is, in principle at least, no difference in the meaning of enharmonically equivalent notes. Which spelling is selected is merely a matter of convenience.[6] In the notation of set-forms in the examples below, each accidental affects only the note before which it stands.)

Some former misconceptions are of interest as curiosities. Postulates 1 and 2 have been grotesquely misinterpreted to imply that "every theme must have twelve notes," an assertion as absurd as would be the analogous statement that in tonal music "every theme must have seven notes." Postulate 2, in spite of evidence to the contrary in almost every bar of Schoenberg's twelve-tone compositions, has been misunderstood to refer to a purely compositional and metrical device: the reiteration of a single note, with none other intervening, a procedure that obviously has no effect whatever upon pitch relations, and that therefore is of no relevance to questions of set-structure.[7] Another serious misunderstanding, and one to which some proponents of the system have contributed, is the confusion of postulate 3 with contrapuntal thematic operations. Postulate 3 simply affirms that intervallic relations between adjacent elements are only temporally affected when the set is inverted, nor is the totality of these relations altered when the original set and its inversion are strictly reversed. At the same time, postulate 3 implies that no other rigorous statement of the set exists, while postulate 4 asserts that transpositions of the set, in any of its four possible aspects, cannot affect the intervallic structure.

The twelve notes of the set derive from a division of the octave into twelve equal parts, a formation that should not be confused with the tempered chromatic scale, even though the resulting elements are respectively identical. The tempered chromatic scale is understood to be a necessary compromise with regard to the tone material of diatonic tonality, providing mere approximations of an infinite series of "real" notes. But where these elements are employed as components of a twelve-tone set one may presumably understand them not as practicable approximations of "real" notes generated by the cycle of fifths, but as "real" notes in themselves, generated by an equal division of the octave. The chromatic scale is still premised upon the perfect fifth as a "natural" referential structure that defines the functional relations, but the

---

[5]"Prime" (in place of "original"), "set-complex," and "transformation" are terms introduced by Babbitt in the unpublished study mentioned in note 2, above.

[6]That is, there is no difference based on criteria that can be deduced from the postulates given above, or that can be shown to have any general relevance to the corpus of music that is known as "twelve-tone music." It is clear, however, that in much of this music certain "voice-leading" or harmonic implications seem to be suggested by the preference for one rather than another spelling in given instances.

[7]See Deems Taylor, *Music to My Ears* (New York: Simon & Schuster, 1949), p. 267.

twelve-tone set does not necessarily presuppose such a criterion of intervallic stability.[8]

An invariant series of intervals, as Schoenberg points out, "functions in the manner of a motive."[9] This ostinato twelve-tone motive, however, differs fundamentally from the tonal motive. A twelve-tone work, in Schoenberg's system, consists of perpetually varied restatements of a twelve-tone set. As a result of compositional operations the set may acquire certain thematic characteristics, distinctive features in contour, rhythm, phrase structure, dynamics, and so forth—features that may transform the abstract series into a more or less tangible thematic formation. At the same time, all the other pitch components of the work are derived from the set. If the set is understood to be a "motive" in itself, in terms of the ordered pitch relations which it presents, how is the "thematic" to be differentiated from the "nonthematic"? What is the context within which the "motive" is manipulated and developed? It is precisely the literal character of the transformations and transpositions of the set that implies its extramotivic function. Were these operations merely motivic, as they are frequently assumed to be, they would not need to be literal. But since they are the different aspects of a single abstract intervallic structure that provides the frame of reference, they can only be literal.

The specific ordering of the notes is a necessary consequence of the concept of the set as a unitary structure whose elements are not functionally differentiated. An unordered twelve-tone set would be equivalent to the semitonal scale, that is, it would be simply a statement of the available tone material. The seven-tone scale may be analogously regarded as a statement of the available tone material of the diatonic system, but in addition, certain functional relations among the elements of the seven-tone scale are implied. Since the elements of the twelve-tone set are not thus functionally differentiated, and since, unlike the seven-tone scale, the set comprises the totality of pitch classes, they must be ordered if the set, conceived as a unitary structure, is to have any constructive significance whatsoever.

Another twelve-tone system was devised by Josef Matthias Hauer.[10] Hauer's set, or "trope," as he terms it, is not a unitary structure but a combination of two six-note segments of mutually exclusive content, within each of which only the content, not the order, is specified. Thus the order in which the notes are

---

[8]The attempts of Schoenberg (see Josef Yasser, "A Letter from Arnold Schoenberg," *Journal of the American Musicological Society,* VI [1953], 53 ff.) and others to derive the twelve notes from the "overtone series" are so farfetched and self-contradictory that they hardly require discussion. Their refutation, however, has no bearing on the musical validity of atonal composition (as H. Schnippering assumes it to have, in his "Atonalität und temperierte Stimmung." *Melos,* XVII [1950], 9 ff., and "Von der Zwölftonmusik," *Melos,* XVII, 312 ff.).

[9]Schoenberg, *Style and Idea* (New York: St. Martin's Press, 1975), p. 219.

[10]J. M. Hauer, *Vom Melos zur Pauke* (Vienna: Universal-Edition, 1925); *Zwölftontechnik* (Vienna; Universal-Edition, 1926).

to be stated is a purely compositional matter, the set functioning only as a means of partitioning the total tone material into specified groups of notes. A similar procedure is employed by Debussy in the Prelude for piano, *Voiles* (see below, pp. 40 f.). With the single exception of two passing notes in bar 31, the outer sections of this work are limited to the notes shown in example 1:

EXAMPLE I

Had the remaining elements of the chromatic scale been employed to define another tonal area, the two hexachords together would have provided an example of one of Hauer's tropes (ex. 2). Since in Hauer's system the set has no preestablished linear structure, there is no question of the aforementioned problematical feature of Schoenberg's system—the relationship of the pre-compositional linear structure of the set to the compositional motive.

EXAMPLE 2

In Hauer's system, as in Schoenberg's, a given set is understood to retain its identity at all transpositions. Postulate 3, however, does not apply: the term "retrograde" can have no precompositional meaning where order is not one of the defining properties of the set; an unordered set may be inverted, but this operation, except in certain special cases (e.g., ex. 2), will revise the relative pitch content comprised within each segment and therefore generate a new trope. Consider the set of Schoenberg's *Third Quartet*, Opus 30. The prime form of this set (ex. 3, *a*) is represented as a trope in example 3, *b*. In order that the inversion of a set may represent the same trope as the prime, one or both of the following conditions must be met: each segment must be capable of inversion without revision of its content; the content of one segment must be statable as the inversion of the content of the other. An inspection of example 3, *b*, establishes the impossibility of either alternative.

EXAMPLE 3

a.

b.

In his later work Schoenberg consistently employs special sets whose segmental content remains invariant under certain operations. For example, the prime set of the *Fourth Quartet* (ex. 4) is inverted as in example 5. The first segment of the prime and the second segment of the inversion are different permutations of the same six notes: consequently an identical relationship exists between the second segment of the prime and the first segment of the inversion. Obviously, such a relationship exists also between the retrograde (obtained by reading ex. 4 backward) and the retrograde-inversion (obtained by reading ex. 5 backward), so that the four aspects of the set are derivable from a single trope. Schoenberg thus combines the two basic, and originally independent, dodecaphonic serial procedures.[11]

EXAMPLE 4

EXAMPLE 5

---

[11]Which system, Schoenberg's or Hauer's, is entitled to the honor of chronological priority will not be considered here. On the origins of twelve-tone music see Herbert Eimert, *Lehrbuch der Zwölftontechnik* (Weisbaden: Breitkopf & Härtel, 1950), pp. 56 ff.; Willi Reich, "Versuch einer Geschichte der Zwölftonmusik," in *Alte und neue Musik* (Zurich: Atlantis Verlag, 1952), pp. 110 ff.; Schoenberg, letter to the New York *Times*, Jan. 15, 1950; Egon Wellesz, *The Origins of Schoenberg's Twelve-Tone System*, a pamphlet published by the Library of Congress (Washington, 1958); Perle and Lansky, "Twelve-Note Composition," in *Grove's Dictionary of Music and Musicians*, 6th ed.; Jan Maegaard, "A Study in the Chronology of Op. 23-26 by Arnold Schoenberg," *Dansk Aarbog for Musikforskning*, 1962, 93 ff. See also Chap. VI, n. 7.

Schoenberg objected to the use of the term "atonality" to designate a musical idiom not based on the traditional tonal functions, recommending in its place "pantonality." The intended implication, presumably, is that the new musical language is a consequence of the merging of all tonalities. But since, according to Schoenberg and his followers, the immediate effect of this supposed merging of all tonalities was the obliteration of the characteristic features of tonality in general, "atonality" would seem to be a more appropriate designation for this language.

Nevertheless, there are certain ambiguities, depending upon how one chooses to define "tonality." Contemporary musical developments have made it evident that triadic structure does not necessarily generate a tone center, that nontriadic harmonic formations may be made to function as referential elements, and that the assumption of a twelve-tone complex does not preclude the existence of tone centers.

Although the term "dodecaphony" is usually restricted to music employing a twelve-tone set, it ought to designate any musical idiom based upon the twelve-tone, or semitonal, scale, including "free" atonality. This term, however, and its equivalent, "twelve-tone music," will be employed here in the customary sense, as having reference to twelve-tone serial composition. Further terminological difficulties arise from the fact that dodecaphonic music is not necessarily strictly atonal, and that it may be tonal either in the sense that traditional elements derived from the major-minor system are consistently employed, such as the triadic harmonies of the Berg *Violin Concerto*, or in the general sense indicated at the end of the preceding paragraph.

The problem of terminology is itself a reflection of the crucial creative problem of our time. For the contemporary composer, as the Devil in Thomas Mann's *Dr. Faustus* puts it, "it is all up with the once bindingly valid conventions, which guaranteed the freedom of play." The dodecaphonist differs from the nondodecaphonist only in his more radical approach to this problem.

II

"Free" Atonality

The "free" atonality that preceded dodecaphony precludes by definition the possibility of a statement of self-consistent, generally applicable compositional procedures.[1] A referential complex of tones may be restricted to a single pitch level[2] in one piece, freely transposed in another, and entirely avoided in a third, even where these are different movements of a single opus. The "rightness" of a particular note depends not upon its possible containment within a preestablished harmonic unit, as it does in tonality, but upon larger compositional factors whose meaning must be discovered within the work itself. Thus an unprecedented degree of ambiguity attaches to the individual progression in general, and this is paralleled on the rhythmic plane by the extreme flexibility of a beat that no longer serves as a support for functional harmonic elements.

A central problem, that of defining the "thematic" material and differentiating it from secondary and transitional material without the benefit of the articulative procedures of tonality, is uniquely presented and solved in each atonal work. Sometimes only certain features of the initially stated pattern retain sufficient individuality to function referentially. In general, the atonal "theme" emerges only in the course of the composition and does not appear as a salient design at the outset of the work, as in tonal music.

The integrative element is often a minute intervallic cell, which may be expanded through the permutation of its components, or through the free combination of its various transpositions, or through association with independent details. It may operate as a kind of microcosmic set of fixed intervallic content, statable either as a chord or as a melodic figure or as a combination of both. Its components may be fixed with regard to order, in which event it may be employed, like the twelve-tone set, in its literal transformations:

---

[1] See Chap. I, pp. 1 and 8.

[2] "Pitch level" refers to placement within the semitonal scale irrespective of octave position.

prime, inversion, retrograde, and retrograde-inversion.[3] (Where it is stated as a simultaneity the order is not generally defined, so that only "prime" and "inversion" are meaningful terms.) Individual notes may function as pivotal elements, to permit overlapping statements of a basic cell or the linking of two or more basic cells.

In example 6 (from *Fünf Klavierstücke*, No. 1, by Schoenberg) the initial three-note motive in the middle voice (*ab-g-bb*) is followed by its retrograde-inversion in bar 3 (*a-c-b*) and accompanied by two statements of the retrograde-inversion in the bass (*a-c-b* and *b-d-c♯*). The content of the initial chord (*ab-a-f♯*) is an inversion of the content of the same motive. In bar 2 a transposition of the original motive appears in the upper part (*eb-d-f*), the association of which with the preceding *f♯* generates another cell (*f♯-eb-d*). The latter is transposed and reversed in the upper part (*d♯-e-g*), retrograde-inverted in bar 3 in the middle voice (*c-b-g♯*), and vertically stated, transposed, at the beginning of bar 4 (*d♯-c-b*). Each of the two basic cells includes the same intervals, a "minor third" and "minor second," but the new juxtaposition of these intervals in the second cell enlarges the total span by a semitone.

EXAMPLE 6

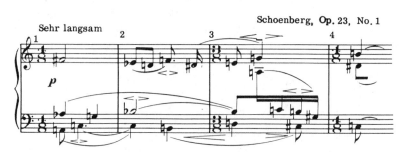

Schoenberg, **Op.** 23, No. 1

Sehr langsam

Copyright 1923 & 1951 by Wilhelm Hansen, Copenhagen.
Used by permission of Wilhelm Hansen.

In example 7, from one of Schoenberg's earliest atonal pieces, *Drei Klavierstücke*, No. 1, the intervallic cell generates a larger, thematically significant pattern.

Rhythm, contour, melodic intervals, and pitch content are treated as separable components of the theme (cf. exx. 7 and 8).

The material that accompanies the theme in example 8, *c*, consists entirely of various transpositions of the inverted form of the initial cell. In example 8, *d*, nonliteral imitations of the original melodic pattern lead to a restoration

---

[3]Unless otherwise defined (Chap. V, pp. 106-108), "inversion" is understood as the complementation procedure described above, p. 3.

of the original notes, but in a new permutation, the recapitulation of the original pitch content functioning as a kind of return to the "home key" and providing an approach to the final chord.

EXAMPLE 7

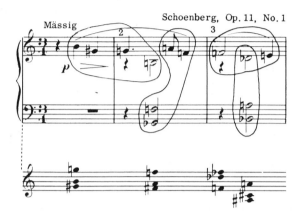

EXAMPLE 8

[cont'd on p. 12]

EXAMPLE 8 [cont'd]

The final chord of the piece (ex. 8, *d*, bar 64) is a verticalized segment of another thematic element (ex. 9, at x), employed throughout at various transpositions but stated at the end in its original "key." At its first appearance (ex. 9) this motive is preceded by a horizontal statement of the initial intervallic cell, transposed, a figure that is chromatically expanded in the next bar (left hand, second beat ff.).

EXAMPLE 9

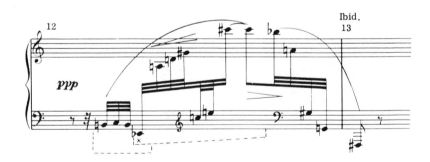

[cont'd on p. 13]

EXAMPLE 9 [cont'd]

In the recapitulation the progression is expanded spatially through octave displacements and telescoped in time (ex. 10).

EXAMPLE 10

The original pitch level of the basic cell (ex. 7) acquires a formal significance in the second theme of the work (ex. 11), the cadential elements of this theme consisting of two intervals, *b-g* and *g♯-b*, that together comprise the pitch-class content of the initial statement of the basic cell.

EXAMPLE 11

[cont'd on p. 14]

EXAMPLE 11 [cont'd]

A new version of the second theme commences with three harmonic elements (ex. 12, at x, y, and z), of which the first is a vertical statement of the basic cell transposed, the second its inversion, and the third an "augmented triad."

EXAMPLE 12

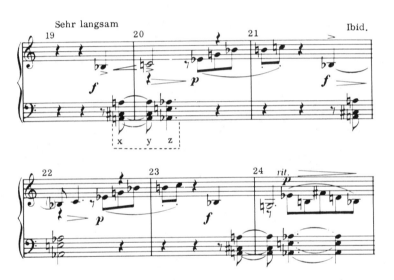

This last element had made several casual appearances earlier. It emerges now as the primary structural detail of a large part of the development section. The important five-note figure of the second theme (see the left-hand part of ex. 11 and the right-hand part of ex. 12) is permuted in bars 23-24, exposing a transposition of the same chord (ex. 12, beginning of bar 24, right-hand part). Associated at this point with the development of the second theme, the "augmented triad" is next (ex. 13) involved in the development of the first theme and of the thematic element illustrated in example 9 (at x):

EXAMPLE 13

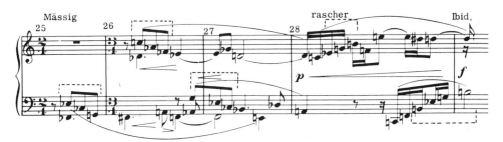

It should be noted that the special property that derives from the uni-intervallic structure of the "augmented triad"—its retention of the same pitch-class content at three different transpositions, equivalent to its harmonic inversions—determines the various transpositions of the thematic elements in example 13. The same principle, in the recapitulation, restores the left-hand figure of the second theme to its original "key" (cf. ex. 11 with ex. 14). All four nonequivalent transpositions of the "augmented triad" appear in the tenth and ninth bars from the end, beginning with the *db-a-f* on the downbeat of the former.[4]

EXAMPLE 14

---

[4]On the second beat of this bar, upper staff, the note on the third space is a misprint for *b♯*. This is verified by the sharp, which is correctly placed on the third line in the editions that preceded the *Gesamtausgabe*. I am indebted to the pianist, Paul Jacobs, for bringing this to my attention. Unfortunately, in the *Gesamtausgabe* the error has been "corrected" by a shift in the position of the sharp, rather than in that of the note.

Chords or melodic patterns derived through operations upon a single intervallic cell are particularly useful in the formulation of unifying procedures,
with respect to both immediate context and the work as a whole. In No. 4 of
Fünf Sätze for string quartet by Anton Webern, presented in its entirety (right)
(ex. 16), a minimal detail, the semitone, is combined first with its transposition at the "perfect fourth," then with its transposition at the tritone, thus
generating the primary elements of the movement (ex. 15, x and y). The
second chord is merely a chromatic expansion of the first, a progression that
generates only a single new note. The important melodic detail, *e-f♯*, consists
of the only notes that are not common to both x and y.

EXAMPLE 15

$$x \quad y \quad\quad x \quad y$$

This melodic detail appears initially in the first violin, bars 1-2, and
subsequently acquires new structural associations in connection with other
elements. It appears as an independent motive in the viola in bar 2, as a
component of a larger melodic pattern in bars 6 and 10, and as a component
of an ostinato figure shared by viola and cello in bars 7-9.

In bar 3 a melodic statement of y is presented in the first-violin part. At the
same time, the notes that are common to both formations, *b-f-c*, are contra-
puntally associated with *e*, the remaining component of x, in the viola. From
the conclusion of bar 3 through the beginning of bar 6, x and y are transposed
and horizontally and vertically reformulated, with overlapping common elements employed as a modulatory means.

The "new" sixteenth-note figure in bar 6 commences with the initial four
notes of the first-violin part, which are thus dissociated from their original
connection with x and y. At the same time, the figure as a whole is a
linearization of elements comprised within the initial transpositions of x and y,
from the conclusion of bar 3 through the beginning of bar 4.

The resulting new relationships are ingeniously exploited in the second
section of the movement, bars 7-9. The first four notes (*c-e-f♯-b*) of the
sixteenth-note motive are inverted at a pitch level (*b♭-g♭-e-b*) that retains
three of the original notes, the inverted formation being embedded in the
ostinato of the three lower instruments. The *d* which appears here in association with *b♭-g♭* forms a new, reiterated pattern in the viola.

The literal transposition in bar 10 of the earlier sixteenth-note motive (bar
6) restores all the notes of bars 1 and 2, but in a new permutation and
associated with a new element, *a*. This new statement of the motive (bar 10)
initiates a kind of abbreviated recapitulation (cf. bar 5, including the pre-

EXAMPLE 16

ceding upbeat, with bars 11-12). The linear progression d-$c\sharp$ in the first violin at the conclusion of bar 5 and in the cello at bar 6 is verticalized in bar 12 (as part of the pizzicato chord) and attracts to itself the remaining elements of y, but in a "key" so remote that the formation now has no notes in common with those contained in y at its original pitch level. The new level of y determines the pitch of a final literal transposition of the special motive of bar 6, a transposition that unexpectedly restores, as the final note of the movement, an important stable element of the beginning, the high $f\sharp$, played *sul ponticello* in the first violin in bars 2 and 3. The direction *sul ponticello* applies to the special motive of bars 6, 10, and 13 only at its final appearance, as a means of associating the final $f\sharp$ with the $f\sharp$ that appeared in the same octave at the beginning of the movement.

The use of highly individualized timbres, spatial relations, and rhythmic and dynamic details is characteristic of Webern and operates in general, as in the work under discussion, to formulate and delimit associations in an idiom wherein harmonic and melodic homogeneity tend to obliterate distinctions. A single sonic detail may operate as a referential element, as, for example, the pizzicato chord in the next to the last bar of example 16, which recalls that of the second bar and emphasizes the recapitulative character of bars 11-12. Specific notes are strategically placed within a phrase—as highest or lowest, first or last—because of some special articulative role assigned to them. Thus, in the present movement, a single note, the $e\flat$ in the cello at bar 1, acquires special importance as the lowest element and is obliquely related to the highest element, $f\sharp$, in the following bar. The same oblique relationship occurs in bars 2-3. In bars 10-11 the $e\flat$ is the concluding note of one phrase, the $f\sharp$ the initial note of the next. Finally, the two are directly juxtaposed as the concluding elements of the movement. Similarly, the e and b in the cello and second violin in bars 7-10 are sustained for a purpose that transcends the immediate moment. Their meaning becomes clear in bar 9, where the pizzicato ostinato figure in the viola disintegrates while the first violin comes to rest upon a sustained c. The chord e-b-c is thus exposed, comprising three of the four notes that constitute x in the "home key." The fourth note, f, follows in the viola, as the initial element of the transposed special motive, whose new pitch level is at the same time specifically predetermined by the largest formal requirements, as explained above. Again, the unexpected regrouping of elements in the first violin part at bar 9—the slurring of $g\sharp$ with c instead of with the preceding b as in bar 8—anticipates the first two notes of the final transposition of the sixteenth-note motive at the conclusion of the movement.

Works in which specific harmonic and melodic details are stabilized at definite pitch levels as referential formations of overall significance—as, for instance, in the two compositions analyzed above—are representative of only one phase of atonal composition. Certain so-called athematic works are governed by the opposite principle, that of nonrepetition. Special elements may be emphasized and isolated by some of the devices described in the preceding paragraph, not as a means of establishing focal points but for the opposite purpose. This procedure has sometimes been described as "perpetual variation." In its usual sense, however, variation implies (1) the presence of some stable referential pattern, however temporary, which is identifiable as the subject and distinguishable from the modifications to which it is subjected, and (2) some delimitation of the range of variational possibilities. Neither of these conditions is characteristic of the athematic style, a kind of musical stream of consciousness wherein the thread of continuity is generated by momentary associations. Microcosmic elements are transposed, internally reordered, temporally or spatially expanded or contracted, and otherwise revised, in a fluctuating context that constantly transforms the unifying motive itself.

In example 17, from Schoenberg's *Erwartung*, chords of alternating tritones and "perfect fourths" dominate the harmonic texture.[5] Repeated formations of fixed pitch-class content, encircled in the example, have only a temporary and local importance in this work and usually occur as brief ostinati in combination with "free" elements. Brief sequential passages are found, with the components of the primary pattern unequally transposed so that the harmonic formation is altered at each repetition of the pattern (ex. 18).

A complete movement may consist of the presentation of variable details against an ostinato. Here the most primitive integrative device, simple reiteration, is applied to a single component of an otherwise "athematic" work. Examples are the second movement of Schoenberg's *Sechs kleine Klavier-*

EXAMPLE 17

Schoenberg, Op. 17 (1909)

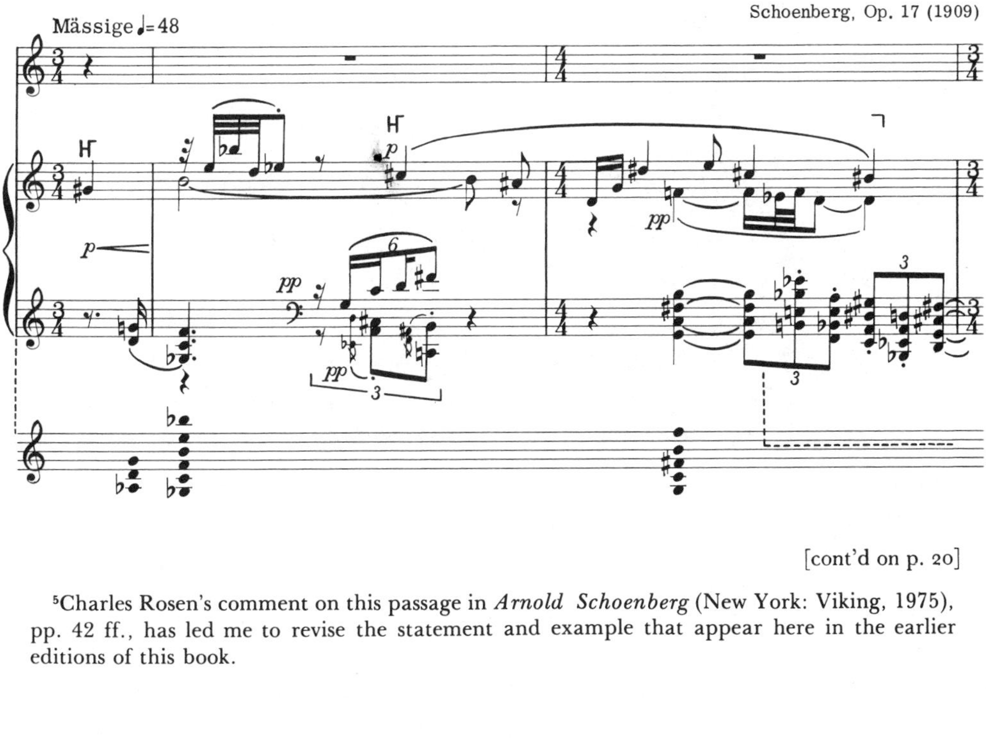

[cont'd on p. 20]

[5] Charles Rosen's comment on this passage in *Arnold Schoenberg* (New York: Viking, 1975), pp. 42 ff., has led me to revise the statement and example that appear here in the earlier editions of this book.

EXAMPLE 17 [cont'd]

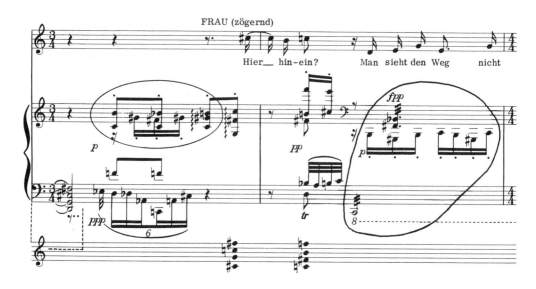

EXAMPLE 18

stücke, Opus 19, the second movement of Berg's *Vier Stücke* for clarinet and piano, Opus 5, and the first and third movements of Webern's *Vier Stücke* for violin and piano, Opus 7.

In the perpetually changing tone weft of the "athematic" style, any recognizably consistent feature, regardless of its brevity, becomes a structural element. The series of "major thirds" in the upper part of example 19, the beginning of *Drei Klavierstücke*, No. 3, by Schoenberg, functions in this way, as does the encircled formation, although stated only twice in the entire composition.

EXAMPLE 19

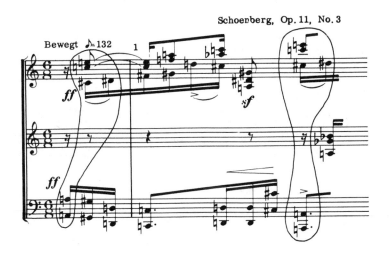

The subtle interrelation of microcosmic elements in an "athematic" work (*Sechs kleine Klavierstücke*, No. 1, by Schoenberg) is illustrated in example 20.

Webern's *Drei kleine Stücke*, Opus 11, for cello and piano, is representative of those works that apply the principle of nonrepetition most radically. Progression is achieved through juxtaposition of minimal elements, with surface reiteration avoided except for isolated and temporary details. The term "athematic" is no more appropriate as a descriptive designation of these works than "all-thematic" would be. Any aspect of a musical idea—melodic contour, harmonic formation, texture, dynamics, rhythm, even the octave position of an individual note—may serve as the momentary referential basis of a non-literal restatement. The extreme brevity of these works is not an idiosyncratic feature but a necessary and logical consequence of the multiplicity of function of every single element.

EXAMPLE 20

Opus 11, No. 3, reproduced in its entirety in example 21, consists only of three short phrases, the pitch-class content of each limited to a segment of the chromatic scale (except for the *f♯* in bar 7), with no note repeated within the phrase.

The first and second phrases are related as antecedent and consequent, through the strategic placement of the only notes they have in common (the isolated initial *e♭* and *f♭* of the trill in the cello part at the beginning, repeated in the piano as the lowest notes at the end of the second phrase; the lowest note of the first phrase—the sustained *f* in the piano, bars 2–3—repeated in bars 5–6 as the highest note of the second phrase and the only one given to the cello). From this point of view the third phrase may be interpreted as a kind of coda. The three notes that are common to the first two phrases (*e♭, f♭, f*) are omitted in the third phrase; the note *a*, the only one of the twelve that has not yet been heard, appears, in the third phrase, for the first time.

From another point of view the form is a free A B A, the first and final phrases each consisting of a single chord in the piano accompanying a linear formation in the cello. The middle phrase is a contrasting section, by virtue of (1) the special sonority of the melodic element, which appears here in the

EXAMPLE 21

Copyright 1924, renewed 1952 by Universal Edition, A.G., Vienna.
Used by permission.

piano part, (2) the absence of each of the notes of this melodic element from the entire cello part, and (3) the appearance of the lowest note of the movement, *e*, and the longest, *g*, at the center of the piece, bars 5–6, together with the single climactic *f* in the cello.

Motivic interrelations are similarly complex and various. The initial four notes of the cello (*e♭-f♭-c-b*) are employed in the piano part as a kind of set (bars 2–4: *d-c♯-f-f♯*; bars 4–6: *g♯-g-c♭-e*). The melodic element of the second phrase, given to the piano, is a permuted imitation of the three-note chromatic segment that concludes the initial phrase of the cello part. The original segment returns as a component of the final chord. The sustained chord at the mid-point of the piece (bars 5–6) includes a transposed vertical statement of the same three notes.

In its harmonic aspect atonal music is especially refractory to analysis. The assertion, frequently made, that the vertical dimension in atonal music is merely a resultant of linear details is an evasion of the problem and, in any case, an overstatement. In atonal works not based upon rigorous contrapuntal procedures there is in general a total interpenetration of harmonic and melodic elements rather than a partial interpenetration of functionally differentiated planes, as in tonal music. I have already shown that, in the works discussed above, what I have designated as the "basic cell" is statable either as a melodic succession or as a simultaneity and is not infrequently the source of obliquely adjacent pitch relations. At the same time, there are independent harmonic entities whose structure and progression cannot be explained by this or any other single concept. It is necessary, above all, to distinguish between harmonic elements that are arbitrarily selected for the particular work and others that are operationally derived.

Even though a functional unit is lacking, several procedures are available that provide the effect of "normal" harmonic continuity within a limited area. Voice-leading through symmetrical movement, repetition, sequence, or chromatic inflection is always "smooth" and a justification for any incidental simultaneity. Moreover, a certain differentiation of material may be obtained through the statement of an independent line against other parts which, by themselves, are absorbed by the above-mentioned means into a homogeneous harmonic formation. These devices may be traced to the development represented by the late nineteenth-century chromaticists and certain preatonal "modernists." The radical aspect of their use in atonal music is in their final dissociation from the concept of root progression. They play an important role in certain works on the borderline of atonality, as, for example, Alban Berg's *String Quartet*, Opus 3. In more advanced atonal compositions they appear as isolated and momentary details, relegated to a minor position in relation to verticalized linear elements and to a freer use of arbitrary harmonic constructions as assumptive details.

A chromatic progression may be direct, as in example 22, or indirect—that is, with octave displacements of inflected elements—as in example 23.

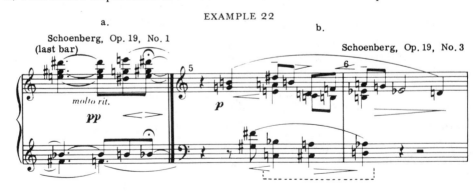

EXAMPLE 22

a.

Schoenberg, Op. 19, No. 1 (last bar)

b.

Schoenberg, Op. 19, No. 3

EXAMPLE 23

Individual voices sometimes depart from an expected chromatic inflection in order to avoid an octave doubling (see discussion on octave doubling, below). The expected movement of the upper voice from *b* to *c* in the piano part, bar 3, of example 24 (from *Vier Stücke* for violin and piano by Webern) is belatedly achieved in bar 4, where the chordal segment in the bass is sustained instead of descending chromatically as before, the octave doubling thus being avoided in both instances.

EXAMPLE 24

Chromatically altered elements may be rhythmically displaced in order to vary the harmony (ex. 25). A more extensive chromatic progression is illustrated in example 26.

EXAMPLE 25

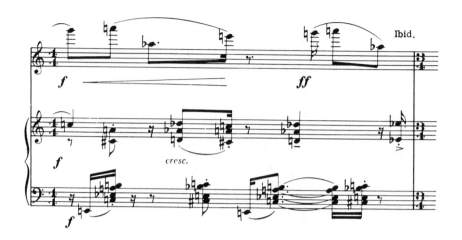

EXAMPLE 26

In example 27 (from *Fünf Sätze* for string quartet by Webern) the chromatic inflection generates a symmetrical chord—that is, a chord that may be analyzed into two segments, one of them the literal inversion of the other. Because of its self-evident structure such a chord tends to have a somewhat stable character, which suggests its employment as point of origin or destination of a harmonic progression (ex. 28, from *Fünf Lieder* by Webern).

EXAMPLE 27

Webern, Op. 5, No. 1 (1909)

EXAMPLE 28

Webern, Op. 4, No. 1 (1908–1909)

The progression itself may be symmetrical, as in example 29 (the concluding bars of the third movement of Berg's *Vier Stücke* for clarinet and piano). The central axis of the symmetrical formation in the quoted passage is the note *d*, which is employed as a kind of "tonic." (Symmetrical formations of the kind illustrated in example 29 occur very infrequently in the works of the atonal school. They are more frequently and significantly exploited in certain works of Bartók, particularly his *Fourth* and *Fifth String Quartets*. See my article "Symmetrical Formations in the String Quartets of Béla Bartók."[6])

---

[6]*Music Review,* XVI (1955), 300 ff. See also Leo Treitler, "Harmonic Procedures in the Fourth Quartet of Béla Bartók," *Journal of Music Theory, III* (1959), 292 ff., and Perle, *Twelve-Tone Tonality,* 10 ff.

EXAMPLE 29

Any harmonic element is automatically justified through literal or sequential reiteration; but these procedures, owing to their obvious character, are rarely applied to a total harmonic formation. Sequence and repetition become generally useful means of harmonic clarification only in connection with such complicating factors as unequal transposition (ex. 18), rhythmic displacement (ex. 25), octave displacement (ex. 30), and the combination of these with other devices and with assumptive details.

Individual chords are sometimes derived by means of operations upon a

EXAMPLE 30

Webern, Op. 4, No. 2 (1908–1909)

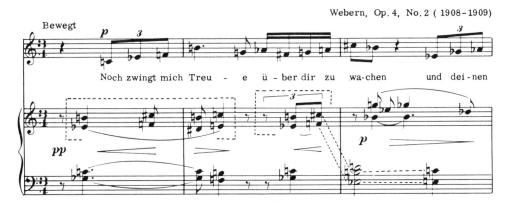

Noch zwingt mich Treu – e ü – ber dir zu wa-chen   und dei-nen

Copyright 1923, renewed 1951 by Universal Edition, A.G., Vienna.
Used by permission.

EXAMPLE 31

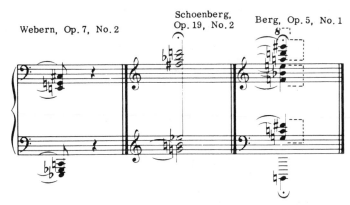

Webern, Op. 7, No. 2 — Schoenberg, Op. 19, No. 2 — Berg, Op. 5, No. 1

chordal segment. Symmetrical chords belong in this category. A chord so derived is likely to occupy a distinctive moment in the movement as a whole. Each of the examples illustrated above (ex. 31) is the final chord of an atonal movement, and each consists of the simultaneous statement of a chordal segment together with one or more transpositions of this segment.

A tendency to avoid the octave is frequently observable in atonal music.[7] The avoidance of the octave as a melodic interval is characteristic of the idiom, but there is considerable variation in its harmonic treatment, ranging from the avoidance of doublings in individual chords to the avoidance of

---

[7] See Schoenberg, *Theory of Harmony* (Berkeley and Los Angeles: University of California Press, 1978), p. 420.

EXAMPLE 32

Copyright 1924, renewed 1952 by Universal Edition, A.G., Vienna.
Used by permission.

oblique octave relations as well. Where a consistently dissonant idiom is essentially generated by linear elements, doubling seems to unbalance the texture and to interrupt the forward thrust. Example 32 illustrates an octave doubling deliberately employed as a momentary, exceptional detail that "resolves" into a "minor ninth," a progression analogous to the suspension in tonal music.

The octave relation in atonal music is only part of a larger problem, that of the evaluation of intervallic quality in general in nontriadic music. Roger Sessions suggests that

the intervals, and their effects, remain precisely the same; two notes a fifth apart still produce the effect of the fifth, and, in whatever degree the context permits, will convey a sensation similar to that of a root and its fifth, or of a tonic and its dominant. A rising interval of a semitone will produce somewhat the effect of a "leading tone," principal or secondary, and so on.[8]

Though specific instances can be discovered in atonal music to support this view, the evidence seems insufficient to justify its acceptance in general. In any event, the special devices by means of which particular relationships are stabilized in atonal music rarely seem to depend upon criteria of this sort.[9]

This is not to deny that each of the different intervals has its own sonic quality or what has been called, for lack of a better term, "degree of tension." In isolation from any compositional context one can evaluate the "degrees of

[8]Roger Sessions, *Harmonic Practice* (New York: Harcourt, Brace and Company, 1951), p. 407.

[9]However, see the second sentence of n. 6, Chap. I, above.

tension" of the intervals from the "minor second" to the tritone as varying inversely with the size of the interval, and of those from the tritone to the "major seventh" (merely the harmonic inversion of the former) as varying directly with the size of the interval. But there is certainly no basis whatever for Ernst Krenek's classification of the intervals in atonal music according to the traditional consonance-dissonance dichotomy.[10] The abandonment of the concept of a root-generator of the individual chord is a radical development that renders futile any attempt at a systematic formulation of chord structure and progression in atonal music along the lines of traditional harmonic theory.

The independence of the linear dimension in atonal music from the restrictive criteria of simultaneity and progression that are characteristic of tonal music has on occasion suggested the employment of a rigorous contrapuntal scheme as a means of organizing a total musical complex. Examples of strict canonic structures are *Fünf Canons*, Opus 16, and the concluding movement of *Fünf geistliche Lieder*, Opus 15, by Webern, and Nos. 17 and 18 of Schoenberg's *Pierrot lunaire*. A problematical aspect of the atonal canon is the determination of the interval that shall separate the canonic voices, for the choice is an arbitrary one where maintenance of key identity is not a requirement. No *general* vertical consideration seems to influence the progress of the individual voices in these works except that of avoiding doublings.

No. 18 of *Pierrot lunaire* is a work of extraordinary complexity in its linear relations. The movement is scored for piccolo, clarinet, violin, cello, *Sprechstimme*, and piano. A three-part fugue unfolds in the piano part, a fugue traditional in motivic elaboration but exceptional in the very large compass covered by each of the voices, which cross one another freely, and in the occasional appearance of additional supporting lines or chords. Although the fugue is a self-contained component of the work, its first two voices in order of entry form strict canons in augmentation with the clarinet and piccolo. At the same time, a third canon, between violin and cello, functions as an accompaniment to the fugue and to the other two canons, in that it does not exploit the salient motivic elements of the other parts. At the exact mid-point of the movement, the clarinet and piccolo, having reached that point at which their canonic associates in the fugue will arrive only at the end of the movement, reverse their direction, so that they form the retrograde in diminution of the two fugal voices. The independent canon in violin and cello is also reversed at this point. Except for occasional nonliteral imitations of fugal motives, the vocal part is free.

In the exposition of the first movement of Schoenberg's *Serenade*, Opus 24, periodicity, dependent in tonal music upon functional harmonic relations, results from the contrapuntal manipulation of a total musical complex rather than of a melodic subject. Thus the whole section comprising bars 1-8 is literally inverted at bars 17-24, and is exactly repeated (except for occasional octave displacements) against new material at bars 9-16, that section being in

---

[10]Ernst Krenek, *Studies in Counterpoint* (New York: G. Schirmer, Inc., 1940), pp. 7 f.

EXAMPLE 33

Schoenberg, Op. 24

turn inverted as a totality at bars 25-32, repeated at bars 33-40, and again inverted at bars 41-48. In the four bars that introduce the middle section of the movement (ex. 33) the prime and inverted forms of the cadential chord of the preceding sections are transposed at the tritone. The reiterated juxtaposition of these two forms of the cadential chord at this point summarizes the formal procedures upon which the exposition is based. A noteworthy detail is the retention, in the outer voices, of g and a and, in the inner voices, of $g\flat$ and $b\flat$, these dyads remaining invariant within the particular set of inversional relations employed.

The independent structural role that rhythm is free to play as a consequence of the dissolution of a functional harmonic unit is illustrated in the second of Webern's *Fünf Canons*. The sole thematic operation within the line itself is found in the condensed recapitulation of the initial rhythmic pattern (ex. 34). The exploitation of rhythm as a separable component of an atonal theme has

EXAMPLE 34

Webern, Op. 16, No. 2 (1924)

already been illustrated (see exx. 7 and 8, *a*). In the famous "Invention on a Rhythm" from *Wozzeck* (Act III, Scene 3) an independent rhythmic pattern functions as the primary referential element.

Melodic and harmonic ostinati that are subjected to systematic rhythmic variation are illustrated in examples 11 and 12. In the right-hand part of the former the two melodic lines are initiated in a new temporal relationship at each repetition (in the first statement the two voices commence simultaneously; in the second the soprano precedes the alto; in the third the alto precedes the soprano). Terminal points, on the other hand, maintain the same temporal relationship at each repetition. But the juxtaposition of these terminal points with the literally repeated left-hand figure presents another pattern of constantly varied temporal relationships. The first termination of the two melodic details in the right-hand part occurs on the third note of the five-note motive, the second termination on its second note, and the third termination on its first note. Right- and left-hand parts together present an aggregate which is literally reiterated in terms of pitch content but durationally expanded at each reiteration through the displacement of its components. In example 12 the second chord in the repeated harmonic pattern in the left hand is progressively lengthened, from a durational value of three, to four, to five eighth notes.

The extreme differentiation of rhythmic details is an integral feature of certain phases of atonal composition. Its purpose is essentially similar to that of other characteristic features and may be deduced from the general discussion above (pp. 18-23). It is evident that, in general, rhythm plays a far more important role than pitch relation in the establishment of phrase structure and cadence in atonal music. It remains to be pointed out that the superficially more sensational innovations in rhythm in certain early works of Bartók and Stravinsky are of an essentially different order from those of the atonal school, being based upon metrical units which, in spite of every irregularity, remain a means of projecting explicit and recurrent harmonic entities. Though the rhythmic innovations of early atonality are less obvious, they are far more radical in their implications, for the general assumption of a norm, departure from which would constitute an irregularity, is eliminated.

The last two examples given above are taken from their authors' final essays in nonserial atonality. Their dependence on formal procedures that predetermine the choice of pitches for large segments of the work is symptomatic of the needs and tendencies that led to the formulation of the twelve-tone system. With the adoption of the latter as an exclusive basis for atonal composition in the works of Schoenberg and his immediate disciples,[11] the period of "free" atonality was seen as a closed historical epoch that necessarily and inevitably had been superseded by a new stage of development. But Schoenberg's twelve-tone system has its source in only a few of the seemingly inexhaustible implications of the music of that period. A study of *Wozzeck* is particularly suggestive in this respect.[12]

Centricity—the stabilization of a specific pitch or collection of pitches as a focal element of the whole or of large segments of a work—is an integrative principle of the greatest significance in *Wozzeck*. I am not referring here to the occasional assertion of traditional diatonic functions, which have been frequently noted by other commentators, but to tone centers that are not generated by diatonic functions and that have a much more explicit overall importance. The primary referential chord of the work (ex. 35) is evolved in the course of the first scene (bars 6, 50, 168-171) and is thereafter explicitly stated only in the concluding bars of each of the three acts and in the prelude to Act II, as part of a special cadential pattern (ex. 36).

Segments of this chord, above all the dyad *b-f*, are independently employed as tone centers. This dyad is a point of orientation throughout the work, in the context of both its largest and its smallest components. The principal pitch level of a number of important leitmotifs is that which exposes the interval of a tritone bounded by *b* and *f* (see, for example, the beginning of Act II, Scene 2). As a segment of the main cadential pattern (ex. 36), the basic dyad is

---

[11]A remarkable aspect of twentieth-century music in the United States was the development of more or less independent atonal tendencies that were not displaced by twelve-tone serialism. See Perle, "Atonality and the Twelve-Note System in the United States," *The Score*, July 1960, 51 ff., and Elliott Carter, "Expressionism and American Music," *Perspectives of New Music*, IV/1 (1965), 1 ff. As regards Berg the above statement should be modified to read, "With the adoption of the twelve-tone system as the nominally exclusive basis for atonal composition. . . ." See pp. 76-78, below.

[12]For a more detailed discussion, see Perle, *The Operas of Alban Berg*, Volume One (Berkeley, Los Angeles, London: University of California Press, 1980), Chapter Five.

EXAMPLE 35   EXAMPLE 36

part of the curtain music at the end of each act, but it is independently associated with the initial and final curtains of many individual scenes as well. Salient melodic and harmonic details, especially at moments of dramatic emphasis, often give special prominence to *b* and *f*. The former has priority over all other pitches in the scene of Marie's murder, and the latter has priority in the complementary scene of Wozzeck's death by drowning. Other constituents of the primary referential chord (ex. 35) are independently employed as tone centers within narrower limits. *C♯*, for instance, is the primary linear focal element of Act I, Scene 1, a status attributable to the various ways in which this pitch is emphasized in that scene—as a registral or temporal boundary, through durational preponderance, and through repetition.

In Act II, Scene 1, basic cells and aggregates of basic cells are systematically employed as a means of defining and interrelating the different harmonic areas of a design analogous to that of the traditional sonata allegro. The most consistent harmonic feature of the movement is the "augmented triad" *c♯-f-a* —a segment of the fixed referential chord whose importance in the prelude that introduces this scene was mentioned above. The superimposition of a conjunct semitone upon any one of the notes of the "augmented triad" generates the basic cell of the principal section (bars 7 ff., restated in a second exposition at bars 60 ff. and recapitulated at bars 128 ff.). This cell is shown at its principal transposition in example 37:

EXAMPLE 37

At the climax of the development section (bars 114 f.), the principal leitmotif of the opera is revealed as a linearization of this cell and is given at a transposition that retains the content of the referential "augmented triad" of example 37 (ex. 38):

EXAMPLE 38

Wir ar - me Leut!

The addition of a single note to the basic cell generates a salient melodic and harmonic motive—the "augmented triad" and the "diminished triad" conjoined through a common boundary tone—of the principal section (ex. 39).

EXAMPLE 39

(bars 7, 60 f., 124 ff.)   (bars 7-10, 128-131)

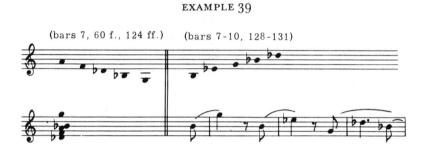

The basic cell of the bridge section, most obviously exploited in the first exposition, bars 29-42, is a "diminished triad" with conjunct semitone superimposed. The primary transposition of this cell (ex. 40) is that which results in maximum intersection with the basic cell of the principal section at the primary transposition of the latter cell (ex. 37):

EXAMPLE 40

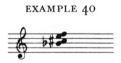

The principal aggregate formation is a five-note collection that comprises the basic cells, in prime and inversion, of the principal and bridge sections. In example 41 this aggregate is illustrated in its "home key," a pitch level which it actually achieves only in the closing section of the recapitulation (bars 162 ff.).

EXAMPLE 41

The inversion of the basic cell of the principal section is equivalent in relative pitch-class content to another basic cell, the "major triad" with conjunct semitone superimposed. This cell is first prominently exposed, at the transposition given in example 42, in the closing section of the first exposition (bars 55-59).

EXAMPLE 42

The subordinate section commences each time (bars 43, 90, 150) with the basic cell shown in example 43:

EXAMPLE 43

The final closing section culminates with this same cell in its "home key," assuming, again, that the latter is to be defined as that pitch level which results in maximum intersection with the basic cell of the principal section as illustrated in example 37 (ex. 44).

EXAMPLE 44

The closing chord of the movement is an aggregate of all four basic cells (ex. 45). Other hexachordal aggregates that may be analyzed into all four basic cells appear elsewhere in the movement, most prominently at the median cadence and at the final cadence (ex. 46) of the first bridge section (bars 29-42).

EXAMPLE 45

EXAMPLE 46

The content of the primary referential chord of the opera (ex. 35) is equivalent to that of a five-note segment of the whole-tone scale plus one "odd" note (ex. 47):

EXAMPLE 47

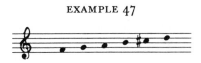

Prominent melodic motives based on such collections are illustrated in example 48.

EXAMPLE 48

Berg, Wozzeck (1922)

Of the two discrete whole-tone scales, that one whose content is completely represented in the primary cadential pattern (ex. 49) is given distinct priority over the other throughout the work:

EXAMPLE 49

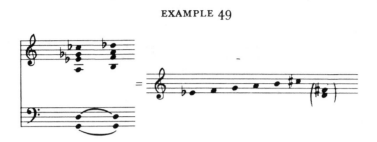

The extent to which such formations are employed as unifying elements is indicated by the fact that the four motives from Act I quoted above all comprise uninterrupted permutations of the same whole-tone segment, g-a-b-c♯-d♯. Both whole-tone scales are exploited most extensively, as a source of harmonic as well as melodic details, in the final symphonic interlude, the principal subject of which is shown in example 48, *f*.

The differentiation of pitch-class collections through the use of whole-tone segments is found in atonal music from its very inception. (An instance from Schoenberg's Opus 11, No. 1, is quoted above, example 8, *a*.) This and other features of atonal music that have been discussed earlier in this chapter are given large-scale structural implications in *Wozzeck*. Chromatic inflection, for instance, generates a chord progression that is not merely an incidental detail, as in example 26, but the structural unit that governs a whole scene and its adjoining interludes (ex. 50).

EXAMPLE 50

Act III

Interlude   Scene 4   Interlude

215 = 218-219   220-319   320   370-371

D

III

Nondodecaphonic Serial Composition

The twelve-tone system is not as insulated from other contemporary musical developments as it is sometimes assumed to be. Essentially, Schoenberg systematized and defined for his own dodecaphonic purposes a pervasive technical feature of "modern" musical practice, the ostinato. The continual reiteration of a musical unit is a primary structural device where tonal functions are undeveloped or ambiguous, in "primitive" as in "modern" music. In serial composition, however, the ostinato is no longer a constantly perceptible surface phenomenon but the musical substructure, the groundwork. Serial procedures[1] have been employed not only by Schoenberg and his disciples but also, independently, by Scriabin, Stravinsky, Bartók, and others.

Debussy's *Voiles*, briefly discussed in Chapter 1, merits a few additional comments. The tone material of each of the three sections of this work is rigorously derived from a restricted selection of the notes of the semitonal scale, defined only with regard to content, not order. The only tonal contrast in the work results from the fact that the set upon which the middle section is based (ex. 51, *a*) is not the same as that of the two outer sections (ex. 51, *b*).

EXAMPLE 51

---

[1]In a strict sense the term "series" denotes an ordered succession of elements, such as the Schoenbergian twelve-tone set. Hauer's "tropes" are only partially ordered, while in the works of Scriabin and some other composers the set is a *collection* of pitches the specific ordering of which is purely compositional. The term "serial composition" is used in the present study as a general designation for music based on any of these types of sets.

Each set functions both as chord and as scale, that is, as the sole criterion of both simultaneity and linear succession.

Scriabin, in his employment of a more complicated set, of transpositions of the set, of invariant segments that function as pivotal elements among the various transpositions, and of consistent variants of the set, may be considered the first to exploit serial procedures systematically as a means of compensating for the loss of the traditional tonal functions.

EXAMPLE 52

The primary set upon which the *Seventh Sonata* is based may be linearly arranged as in example 52 (the spelling is Scriabin's). In the course of the work the second degree of this scale is sometimes raised a semitone, the fourh sometimes lowered a semitone. These modifications, the only ones permitted, provide what might be described as "modal" variants. As a self-sufficient chordal formation the set may be spelled as either a series of thirds or a series of fourths (ex. 53). The famous "mystic chord" of *Prometheus* (ex. 54) may be derived from example 53, *b*.

EXAMPLE 53   EXAMPLE 54

The most significant compositional element is the chordal segment consisting of the upper four notes of the unmodified version of example 53, *a*. This segment and its transposition at the minor third above are both derivable from a single statement of the set, a possibility that permits the establishment of a closed system of transpositions and a principle of progression. The pivotal function of the segment is in this respect analogous to that of the triad in the major-minor system. (See ex. 55, *a*. The level of transposition is indicated by the symbol "T" followed by an arabic numeral signifying the degree of the semitonal scale to which the set is transposed with reference to the original pitch level of the set, indicated by "T-0.") Another pivotal formation is the "diminished-seventh" chord, comprising the only notes common to all four members of the transpositional complex illustrated in example 55 (see ex.

55, *b*). Of importance in its connection with larger formal elements is the group of notes comprising the tritone relationships within the set, the invariance of which at the transposition of a tritone results in a six-note segment common to any two sets a tritone apart (ex. 55, *c*).

EXAMPLE 55

The compositional exploitation of these common set-segments is illustrated in examples 56-58.

EXAMPLE 56

Scriabin, Seventh Sonata, Op. 64 (1911)

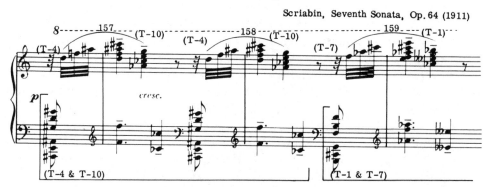

EXAMPLE 57

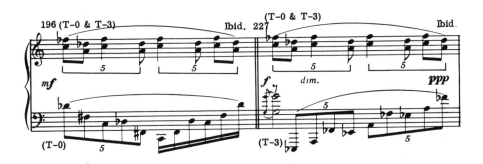

EXAMPLE 58

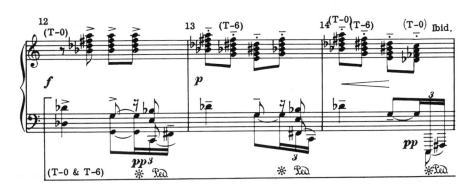

In his *Trois Compositions* for piano, the Russian composer Nicolai Roslavetz employs an independent set for each movement (see ex. 59, in which the sets are given in Roslavetz' own spelling). As in Scriabin's works, the set functions simultaneously as scale and chord. Transpositions are used much more freely, pivotal connections being employed, in general, merely as a means of immediate association. The larger formal implications of controlled transpositional relations are realized to a limited extent in the return of the respective sets to their original pitch level at the conclusion of the second and third pieces and in the derivation of the concluding bars of the first piece from transpositions of the set that are closely related in pitch content to the original statement of the set.

EXAMPLE 59

Variants of the set are more or less consistently employed. These are derived not through the chromatic inflection of set-elements, as in Scriabin's *Seventh Sonata*, but through the systematic omission of certain components of the basic formation. In the third piece, for instance, the third degree of the scalewise arrangement of the set (ex. 59, *c*) is omitted from four successive statements of the set (ex. 60).

EXAMPLE 60

Roslavetz, Trois Compositions, No. 3 (1914)

In the works discussed above, the set functions essentially as a harmonic structure, determining linear relations only so far as it is employed as a "broken chord." But where the *order* of the notes is precompositionally defined, as in Schoenberg's twelve-tone rows, the set functions essentially as a linear structure. Ordering is a specifically Schoenbergian concept and plays a certain role even in the earliest "free" atonal compositions, at least to the extent that the content of the "basic cell" depends upon whether that cell is stated in its prime or in its inverted aspect (see ex. 7).[2]

In Schoenberg's *Fünf Klavierstücke*, Opus 23, one of the immediate precursors of the "strict" twelve-tone system, the first movement is based upon ordered successions that are thematic in scope and function but that nevertheless operate independently of rhythm and other thematic attributes. The derivation of the opening bars from two basic three-note motives was illustrated in the preceding chapter (ex. 6). The larger linear patterns thus generated are subjected to variations in contour, rhythm, dynamics, and so

---

[2]The relationship between the primary form and the literal inversion of an atonal chord is described by Rufer (*Composition with Twelve Notes,* pp. 128 f.) as one that "approximately corresponds to the relationship between [the major and minor triads] in tonal music." This is a typical example of the extravagant analogies that many apologists advance in order to "justify" twelve-tone procedures. It is true that the notes *c-e-g* are a literal inversion of the notes *c-a♭-f,* but tonal chords are derived from roots and are related to key centers, and are not generated by literal inversions.

on, in the course of the work, but the original pitch-adjacencies within the pattern are not modified, except through octave displacement and verticalization (see exx. 6 and 61).

Verticalization (cf. the upper staff of bar 30, ex. 61, with the sixteenth-note figure in bar 3, ex. 6) represents a fundamental concept of atonal composition —that any group of notes which is statable in horizontal succession is also statable as a simultaneity (see p. 24), a concept sometimes designated by the rather questionable term, "vertical melody." Certain problematical aspects of this concept are discussed in detail in Chapter V. For the time being it will suffice to point out that "vertical melody" does not operate as a limiting principle, and that it is only one among many, generally unformulated, criteria of harmonic propriety. In this respect the works of Schoenberg and his followers differ radically from those of Debussy, Scriabin, and Roslavetz discussed above, wherein *every* simultaneity consists of the whole or of a segment of the set.

EXAMPLE 61

Copyright 1923 & 1951 by Wilhelm Hansen, Copenhagen.
Used by permission of Wilhelm Hansen.

The ordered linear formations of Opus 23, No. 1, with the exception of a single retrograde statement in the left-hand part of bars 30-31, are given exclusively in their prime aspect and at a single pitch level, in contrast to the generating cells of the first three bars. Transpositions and transformations of the set are freely employed in Opus 23, No. 3, which is based upon a five-note set that functions both as a compositional motive (the original contour of the set being preserved wherever the ordered succession of pitch relations is maintained) and as an unordered collection. Since the unordered collection is employed in both the prime and the inversion, its relative content is not fixed.

Hereafter the term "unordered set" will designate such a collection whether this collection is employed both in the prime and inversion, as above, or only in a single aspect, as in the works of Scriabin; for in neither case is a specified *succession* of the notes assumed to be a defining characteristic of the set. Where such a succession is assumed, the set is "ordered." The following symbols are employed in subsequent discussions of set-operations: "P," "R," "I," and "RI," to signify the respective transformations—prime, retrograde, inversion, retrograde-inversion—of an ordered set; "P" and "I" for the transformations of an unordered set where it is employed as an invertible structure; the integers 0 to 11 to signify the degree of the semitonal scale to which the set is transposed, "I-0" standing for the inverted set whose initial note is identical in pitch-class with the initial note of the original set, "P-0." The untransposed retrograde versions of "P-0" and "I-0" are indicated by the symbols "R-0" and "RI-0," respectively.[3]

The derivation of the opening bars of Opus 23, No. 3, is illustrated in

EXAMPLE 62

Copyright 1923 & 1951 by Wilhelm Hansen, Copenhagen.
Used by permission of Wilhelm Hansen.

---

[3]Retrograde-related pitch-class successions that have the same transposition number are thus different permutations of the same collection of pitch classes and maintain the same pitch-class adjacencies. However, the assignment of the same transposition number to P and I forms that commence with the same note, and to R and RI forms that end with the same note, is arbitrary, a matter of convenience only; it does not necessarily imply any special connection between the respective collections other than the trivial one of a common boundary note.

example 62. (Motivic set-statements are bracketed in the example.) In spite of the brevity of the set itself, the complexity and ambiguity of its treatment result in a multitude of independent linear and harmonic elements, and these are combined with other elements that are apparently not based on the set at all; therefore the relationship between the set and the musical details that one can ex post facto derive therefrom is generally problematical.

A group of set-relations presented earlier in the movement is exploited in a rigorous and logical manner in the concluding bars. P-0 is here coupled with I-11, and P-7 with I-4. The notes *c* and *g*, missing from both pairs of sets but symmetrically related to each, occur as an invariant element (ex. 63).

EXAMPLE 63

The invariant succession of notes that the ordered prime set shares with its retrograde-inversion at T-7 is occasionally employed as a pivotal device (ex. 62, bars 1-2; ex. 64).

EXAMPLE 64

In Opus 23, No. 4, the multifarious associations that each note acquires tend to negate the integrative possibilities that presumably motivate the employment of serial procedures in the first place. The referential formation (ex. 65) consists of five overlapping sets, four of which comprise harmonic as well as linear elements.

EXAMPLE 65

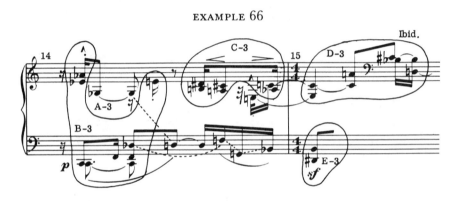

A derived passage, of less than usual complexity, is illustrated in example 66. (Each of the sets is here stated at T–3.)

EXAMPLE 66

The remaining movements of Opus 23 are based upon a more rigorous and consistent exploitation of ordered serial relations. No. 5, in fact, is strictly derived from an ordered twelve-tone set and therefore does not lie within the purview of the present chapter. No. 2, a work of concentrated power and logic and one of the most effective of Schoenberg's creations, is based upon a set that implies within its own structure a variety of possible ordered formations. The set consists of two linear patterns that are stated simultaneously in the first bar of the movement. One of these is the principal series of nine nonrepeated notes, the other a three-note figure the content of which is duplicated in the principal series. The pitch relations that result from the simultaneous presentation of these two elements provide a range within which revisions of the original ordering may occur without destroying the referential function of the set. The original statement of the set and some of the variations to which it is subjected are illustrated in example 67.

EXAMPLE 67

The initial appearance of the set, in bar 1, is followed by five bars of independent expository material (ex. 69, bars 2-6), divided primarily by rhythmic and dynamic means into two sections, which are designated here as *A* (bar 2 to the first beat of bar 5) and *B* (bars 5-6). The exposition concludes, at bar 7, with the first restatement of the set. There follow two bars based on the content of *B* and a sequential passage (bars 10-13) based on a series of successive transpositions of the set (P-0, P-7, P-2, P-9, P-6, P-4). The first four bars of the movement, comprising the set and the *A* theme, are recapitulated in the original "key" in bars 14-17. The final six bars (18 ff.) have the character of a coda. They are strictly derived from the set, employed here for the first time in other than its prime aspect (ex. 68).

EXAMPLE 68

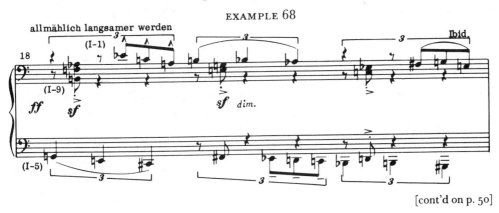

[cont'd on p. 50]

EXAMPLE 68 [cont'd]

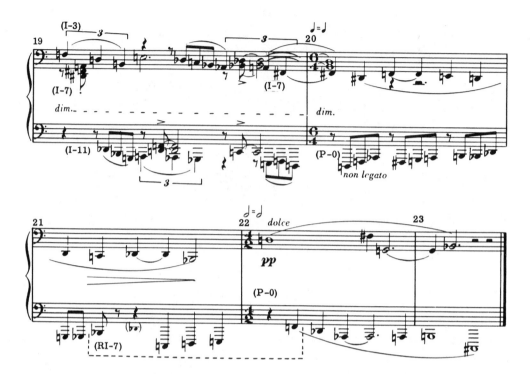

In these concluding bars the set unfolds simultaneously in several transpositions and aspects, a procedure that anticipates one of the fundamental polyphonic principles of dodecaphonic composition. Each half-note value in bars 18–19 comprises the same set of rhythmic elements, the notes being rhythmically deployed in such a manner that corresponding three-note segments of three simultaneous versions of the nine-note set are combined within the duration of each half-note value. A new aggregate of nine pitch classes is thus formed, which functions in these two bars as an unordered set, consisting of the components of three "diminished triads" at the relative pitch levels of T–0, T–4, and T–8. This aggregate is reiterated or transposed at each restatement of the rhythmic set.

The set is subjected to another type of segmentation at its first appearance by means of the rhythmic groupings that coincide with the duration of each note in the left-hand part and through imitation of the contour of the initial four-note figure in the right-hand part (ex. 69, bar 1). These details function as elements of continuity between the first statement of the set and the independent expository material in bars 2–3.

EXAMPLE 69

Rhythm is perhaps the principal propulsive and structural factor in the work as a whole. The progressive diminution of durational values in the left-hand part of bar 3 (including the preceding upbeat) creates a rhythmic intensification that parallels the dynamic intensification of the same bar. Durations of silence are similarly manipulated, as for example, the rests which separate the sixteenth-note groups in bars 1–2 and 14–15. There is a complex interplay of variant and invariant rhythmic details, as in the right-hand part, bars 5–6 (ex. 69), to cite only a single instance. The larger formal elements are likewise characterized by rhythmic means: the main rhythmic details in the exposition are based on interrupted successions of sixteenth notes, in the "modulatory" middle section (bars 10 ff.) on an uninterrupted succession of sixteenth notes, in the last seven bars on a progressive augmentation of the smallest durational value. The separable character of the rhythmic component is illustrated in bars 18–19 (ex. 68), the outer voices of which form noncoincident rhythmic and melodic canons, a procedure that calls to mind the relationship between *talea* and *color* that sometimes occurs in the isorhythmic motet of the Gothic period.

Schoenberg's Opus 24, *Serenade*, may be regarded as a companion piece to

Opus 23 with respect to its historical position as a bridge between the "free" atonal idiom and the twelve-tone system. Like Opus 23, it comprises various experiments in serial composition, not all of which proved fruitful in the course of Schoenberg's subsequent development. The most consistent employment of a nondodecaphonic set is found in the third movement, "Variationen." In the fourth movement, "Sonnet," the vocal solo is rigorously derived from an ordered twelve-tone set, employed, as in Opus 23, No. 5, without transformation or transposition. The instrumental parts derive their material more freely from the same set. The middle section of the fifth movement, "Tranzscene," employs a bisected twelve-tone set, each segment of which preserves its identity only in terms of its content (see exx. 134 and 135).

Serial methods have been almost entirely identified with the atonal school since their systematic formulation in twelve-tone composition, beginning in 1923. There are, however, several more recent instances of the significant use of sets in works that originate outside this tradition. An early example is the first movement of Bartók's *Fourth Quartet* (1928), which employs two unordered four-note sets (ex. 70, x and y), in conjunction with other basic cells as well as tonal and modal elements.

EXAMPLE 70

The sets function not only in their customary role as generators of linear and harmonic details but also as complex "tone centers" — that is, as points of origin and destination and as relatively stable harmonic elements. A linear version of x (ex. 71) is the principal motive of the work as a whole.

EXAMPLE 71

Linear and harmonic derivatives of x and y are respectively illustrated in examples 72 and 73.

Since each set is a symmetrical structure, its content cannot be revised through inversion. The simultaneity x at T-0, however, normally progresses

EXAMPLE 72

EXAMPLE 73

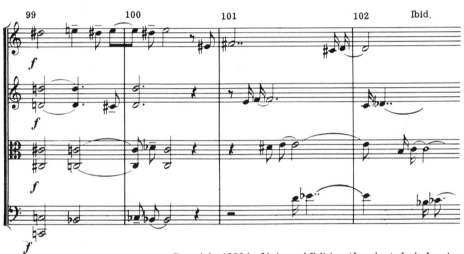

into y at T-0 (ex. 70), resulting in a nonsymmetrical aggregate whose content is revised when the progression is inverted (ex. 74). Toward the conclusion of the movement (bars 152-156) this possibility is realized through the employment of the complement of the original progression.

EXAMPLE 74

The concept that invariant elements may be used as a means of providing pivotal connections among various transpositions of the set has been presented earlier. The uni-intervallic structure of each of the two sets employed in the work under discussion permits a special application of this principle. Either set may be transposed in terms of its own intervallic components — set x by semitones, set y by whole tones — to generate a system of transpositional relations that are analogous, in a sense, to those that occur in the diatonic system through successive transpositions at the perfect fifth. The "key" relations of the present work and their determination by formal considerations support this analogy. Set x is first stabilized at a new pitch level at the conclusion of the exposition (bars 46–49), where it occurs, so to speak, in its "dominant key," T-1, which revises its original content by only one note. The development section commences (bars 49–50) with a transposition of the original x-y progression (ex. 70) to T-2, the "dominant key" of set y. At the conclusion of the development section (bars 85–92) a linear version of set x in the "remote key" of T-3 works its way downward, through successive semitonal transpositions, to the "home key," T-0, at which point the recapitulation commences. (These procedures cannot be properly evaluated independently of other devices, particularly the operation of "axes of symmetry.")[4]

In his later compositions Stravinsky made extensive use of serial procedures. His method prior to the composition of *Canticum Sacrum* is to be distinguished in two important respects from those described up to this point: the employment of the set exclusively in the linear dimension and its derivation from or, at the least, orientation to diatonic formations.

The earliest example is the "Ricercar II" from the *Cantata* (1952). Since, in addition to the considerations just mentioned, what is termed the "set" is in this movement constantly associated with extraserial elements and, with some exceptions, retains the motivic contour of its initial statement, it might conceivably be regarded merely as the compositional motive. It should be observed, however, that (1) the "motive" in this work is defined only in terms of pitch elements, its rhythmical guise being constantly transformed; (2) the transformations and transpositions of the set (with some exceptions — bar 1, p. 18; bars 1–4, p. 22) are literal (see Chap. I, p. 5); (3) a typical serial procedure is represented by occasional nonmotivic statements of the set, involving revisions of the original motivic contour through octave displacements of individual notes. (Such octave displacements are to be found in earlier works of Stravinsky's, as, for example, the middle movements of the *Octet* and the *Symphony of Psalms.*[5])

In the *Septet* (1953) Stravinsky employs a set as the precompositional and

---

[4]See pp. 27 f.

[5]See also Donald C. Johns, "An Early Serial Idea of Stravinsky," *Music Review,* XXIII (1962), 305 ff.

extramotivic basis of a movement for the first time. The set still often appears in the guise of a "theme," but its nonthematic aspects are not less important. Of the three movements of the work, all of the third and almost all of the second are derived from a single set. The first movement, entirely nonserial, anticipates the set in certain of its motives and establishes the key center, *a*, which governs each of the movements. The second movement is a passacaglia, of which the theme (ex. 75) and every other element are rigorously derived from the set, with the exception of a special two-part counterpoint in variations I, IV, and VII.

The passacaglia theme (ex. 75), an eight-bar presentation of the set, is restated in each variation in its prime aspect and original transposition. The final note of this form of the set is the "tonic," *a*. Other special devices that are employed to impart the function of a key center to this note are necessitated by the extremely dissonant harmonic idiom and generally ambiguous tonal context. For example, at its initial presentation, unaccompanied, the theme is divided into several minute segments and distributed among various instruments, only a single doubling occurring, at the penultimate *a* of the set (ex. 75, bar 6); toward the end of variation III (*Septet*, p. 15) the contrapuntal elaboration consists of the exactly simultaneous statement of P-0 and I-10, followed by that of R-0 and RI-10, a procedure that generates doublings only at those points in the set where the note *a* occurs. Were the tritone of this note also a component of the set, this procedure would result in the doubling of that element as well. The absence of this tritone relation is a clue to the tonal intention that underlies Stravinsky's serial method in this work.

EXAMPLE 75

It is interesting to observe, incidentally, that the referential character of the passacaglia theme itself is preserved by a reversal of the technique that prevailed in the previously cited movement of the *Cantata*, in which the exact contour of the motive was generally retained and its rhythm constantly altered. Except in the last two variations, the eight-bar passacaglia theme is reiterated in its original rhythmic form, while its melodic shape is revised each time by means of octave displacements.

The concluding movement, "Gigue," consists of a cycle of four fugues. The set is employed as both an ordered and an unordered formation, generating, in the ordered formation, the thematic material, and in the unordered the counterpoint. In terms of its content the set is reducible to an eight-note scale comprising two identical tetrachords a fourth apart. As in compositions based on the diatonic scale, transpositions at the perfect fourth or fifth result in a literal duplication of one or the other tetrachordal component of the scale. Moreover, the symmetrically inversional structure of both the initial and final six-note segments results in hexachordal invariance between any statement of the set and two transpositions of its inversion (for instance, between P-0 and its inversions at T-0 and T-7). The totality of these relationships may be regarded as a hierarchy of transpositional levels analogous to that of the diatonic system, even being based, like that system, on the circle of fifths (ex. 76). The transpositional scheme employed in the movement is suggested by these pre-compositional connections.

EXAMPLE 76

The spontaneity of Stravinsky's next essay in serial composition, the first and second movements of *Three Songs from William Shakespeare* (1953), for mezzo-soprano, flute, clarinet, and viola, is in marked contrast to the rigorous formalism of the *Septet*. In the first song, several forms of the four-note set are linearly combined into larger quasi-serial formations (ex. 77). (Ex. 78, *a*, is an analysis of the instrumental part of bars 35–43, ex. 78, *b*, an analysis of the instrumental part of bars 14–21). No more than two statements of the set ever appear at one time, one linear concatenation of set-forms unfolding in the vocal part simultaneously with another that is distributed among the three instrumental parts. The only nonserial element in the movement is a diatonic scale-segment that occurs in the introductory and concluding bars, simultaneously with serially generated elements.

The set of the second song, like that of the final movement of the *Septet*, functions as both an ordered and an unordered formation, reducible, in terms of its content, to a scale of two identical tetrachords (conjunct this time, so

EXAMPLE 77

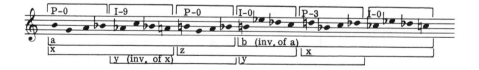

EXAMPLE 78

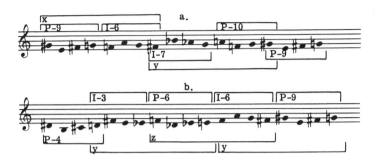

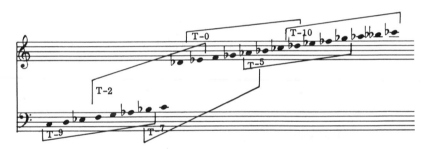

that there are only seven notes) at the distance of a perfect fourth. There is thus, again, a hierarchy of transpositional relationships based on the circle of fifths, a closed system simpler than that of the preceding work, since both the prime set and its inversion comprise the identical pitch content (P-0 is equivalent to I-10, etc.). The transpositions employed constitute a continuous portion of this closed system, as illustrated in example 79.

EXAMPLE 79

(T-9, the most remote transposition employed, occurs but once, at the midpoint of the piece, in the clarinet part under the line "But doth suffer a Seachange." The probability of a programmatic intention here is supported by other, more obvious instances of "tone painting": the exceptional octave displacements in the flute part at "Into something rich and strange"; the five sustained *sforzando* notes in the viola part, bar 1, supporting the first line of the poem beginning "Full fathom five . . ."; a single unordered appearance of the set in the first song, underscoring the part of the text italicized in the following lines: "If the true concord of well-tuned sounds, By Unions mar*ried do offend* thine ears"; the unison between voice and viola at the word "singlenesse" in the first song, bar 31; etc.)

Bar 1 of the second song is derived from the unordered set at T-0 and T-7, bars 16–17 from the unordered set at T-0, bars 18 to the end from the unordered set at T-7, bars 2–15 (with the exception of a few unordered interpolations) from various transpositions of the ordered set. A few isolated chromatic alterations occur (in the clarinet part, bars 16 and 17, and in the viola part, bars 18, 19, and 21).

An analysis of these works must go beyond a mere description of serial operations if it is not to neglect many important integrative devices, particularly in the harmonic field. It is, in fact, impossible to determine the significance of the immediate choice of set-form otherwise. It should be noted that in the present composition the initial harmonic aggregate, *bb-c-eb-f*, is also the one with which the movement concludes. Independent harmonic focal elements perform an especially important and complex role in Stravinsky's next serial composition, *In Memoriam Dylan Thomas* (1954).

The work consists of a "Prelude" for trombone quartet and string quartet, a "Song" for tenor and string quartet, and a "Postlude," which returns to the material and instrumentation of the first movement. All three movements employ the same five-note set. The second movement commences with a phrase (ex. 80) that occurs seven times, rhythmically revised at each repetition. A single harmonic formation serves as both the initial and the final chord of this phrase. Overlapping of successive statements of the set, as in the cello part of example 80, is freely employed.

EXAMPLE 80

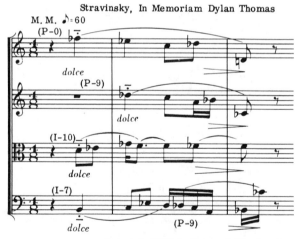

Copyright 1954 by Boosey & Hawkes, Inc.
Used by permission.

The two instrumental groups of the outer movements perform antiphonally, the ritornello to which the strings are restricted in the first movement (ex. 81) being given to the trombones in the third (with some octave transpositions, of course). Each of the three set-forms that appear in the lower voices of example 81 is a different permutation of the identical group of notes. The set-form in the uppermost part, combined with the remaining voices, expands the total

EXAMPLE 81

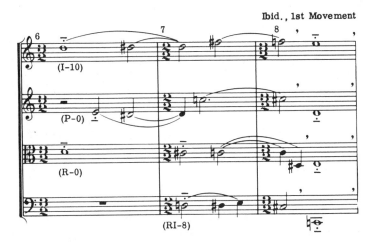

pitch content of the passage into a (compositionally significant) chromatically filled tritone.

The final chord of the ritornello and of the work as a whole (*c-d-e*) consists of the "diatonic" components of the original prime set and is a symmetrical expansion of the single note with which the ritornello commences. It is noteworthy that the passages antiphonally opposed to the ritornello in the first movement enter successively on each of the three notes of this chord, commencing on *e*, *d*, and *c*, in turn. In the Postlude the strings recapitulate, at the "major second" below and the "minor seventh" above, first the second "dirge-canon" of the Prelude and then the first. The respective initial notes are thus converted into *c* and *d*. With the exception of the concluding chord of the work, which is given to both instrumental groups, and the overlapping of the initial *d* of the concluding episode in the strings and the final chord of the ritornello which precedes this episode, the two antiphonal groups are heard together only where the initial *d* of the ritornello coincides with the final chord of the opposed instrumental group, this chord invariably consisting of the notes of a triadic formation (successively "E major" and "E minor" in the Prelude, "D minor" and "D major" in the Postlude).

The relative autonomy of the linear and vertical planes is preserved in these works in spite of the coordination of melodic and harmonic details. In this respect Stravinsky's serial works have nothing in common with the above examples from Debussy, Roslavetz, and Scriabin, wherein the total lack of differentiation between harmonic and melodic material reduces the melodic dimension to what might more aptly be characterized as "horizontal harmony." Nor does Stravinsky employ, in these, the earliest of his serial works, the Schoenbergian device of "vertical melody," the simultaneous statement of elements that happen to be contiguous in the horizontally ordered set, as he does in the later works in which he first employs dodecaphonic series.[6]

---

[6]For a study of these see the articles of Claudio Spies in *Perspectives on Schoenberg and Stravinsky*, ed. by Benjamin Boretz and Edward T. Cone (New York: Norton, 1972).

IV
Motivic Functions
of the Set

A mere description of the set and the transpositions and transformations to which it is subjected cannot be advanced as an "explanation" of the work itself but only of the substructure, the system of tone relations upon which the work is based. Many of the procedures discussed in connection with "free" atonal composition continue to operate, but with the important distinction that they may now be related to a single all-pervasive primary formation. The presence of a stable element in the substructure provides a new basis for the concepts of "nonrepetition" and "perpetual variation" (see pp. 18f.), since the continual reiteration in a twelve-tone work of a single intervallic pattern generally renders literal surface restatement redundant.

A twelve-tone work may be described as a series of variations of an ostinato motive. Such a description, however, characterizes the work only at its most elementary level. An ordered set, according to Schoenberg, "functions in the manner of a motive," but at the same time "it is invented to substitute for some of the unifying and formative advantages of scale and tonality."[1] The interdependence of the motivic and the extramotivic functions of the set is a major compositional issue (see p. 5) that has been regarded from many different points of view by twelve-tone practitioners. A work may be based upon thematic elements derived from the set by means of devious and complex operations that do not necessarily imply a serial context. Thematic elements directly derived from the set may be employed, once so derived, more or less independently of the set. Or the set may be employed as a thematic element in itself. Again, all the linear details may be directly derived from the set without their functioning as "themes" in any traditional sense, as in many of the works of Webern.

I. THE SET AS A THEME

The abstract series acquires the character of a theme when it is consistently differentiated from its "background," which, in the strict twelve-

---

[1]Schoenberg, *Style and Idea*, p. 219.

tone system, is also derived from the set. In order to compensate for the absence of an organic principle of differentiation between the horizontal and vertical planes, such as operates in the diatonic system, the rhythmic structure of the theme is emphasized as a primary attribute. Thematic contrast and development are likewise dependent upon rhythm, and upon secondary features such as texture and dynamics, to a far greater extent than in tonal music. Schoenberg's *Fourth Quartet*, Opus 37, and his *Concerto for Piano and Orchestra*, Opus 42, may be cited among numerous examples of works that employ straightforward melodic statements of the four aspects of the set as expository material.

EXAMPLE 82

The initial thematic idea of the *Concerto* is illustrated in example 82. The immediate repetition of a set-segment, as in bars 5–6, is not generally regarded as a violation of postulate 2 (see p. 2). The assumptions that underlie the freer treatment of the set in the accompaniment are explained in section III of this chapter. (It is often useful to indicate the predetermined temporal positions of the elements of an ordered set. For this purpose the "order numbers" 0, 1, 2, 3, . . . 11 are employed here always in this sequence regardless of the aspect of the set.)[2]

_____

[2]The term "order numbers" and the numerical notation given above are borrowed from Milton Babbitt, *The Function of Set Structure in the Twelve-Tone System*. See p. 2, n. 2.

The treatment of the thematic set is frequently based upon the axiomatic transformation procedures described in Chapter I (postulate 3), which in this case actually function as thematic operations (see p. 4). The employment of the set in this way is illustrated in examples 83 and 84. The anticipation of an element of the set, as at the beginning of example 84, is not uncommon.

Thematic statements of the set may be modified by means of cyclical permutations, as in example 85, in which the thematic character is seen to reside primarily in the rhythmic configuration of the thematic set. Schoenberg's *Quintet for Wind Instruments*, Opus 26 (ex. 86), is based upon a set

EXAMPLE 83

EXAMPLE 84

EXAMPLE 85

Berg, Lyric Suite, 1st Movement

EXAMPLE 86

Schoenberg, Op. 26, 4th Movement

that is cyclically permuted to produce an approximate transposition of the
theme originally derived from the set. In the third movement of Berg's *Lyric
Suite* (ex. 87) three transpositions of P are each presented in a different
cyclical permutation so as to permit each to commence with the same collection of four notes.

EXAMPLE 87

Berg, Lyric Suite 3rd Movement

[cont'd on p. 64]

EXAMPLE 87 [cont'd]

II. THE SET AS A "MELODIC PROTOTYPE"

Even where the set in itself is not employed as a theme, it remains the source of the motivic material of a composition, serving, to quote Ernst Krenek, to

establish a common denominator for all the melodic phenomena of a composition. The utmost degree of coherence, of mutual relatedness of the single elements, being one of the chief artistic aims of Schoenberg and his followers, there was only one step from bringing the independently invented motives of a composition into close relationship to creating first a melodic prototype which would comprise the whole available material in a characteristic pattern, allowing the derivation of the individual motives from that pattern, in which their relatedness would be ascertained by their originating in a common matrix.[3]

The set as a "melodic prototype" can be studied most profitably at this point in a monophonic work, and Krenek's *Suite for Violoncello Solo*, Opus 84, is a suitable illustration. Musical phrases in this work rarely coincide in extent with that of the set, as they usually do in the later works of Schoenberg. The set is instead conceived as a cycle, evidence of the priority of the initially chosen sequence, order numbers 0 to 11, usually occurring only where one set-form is supplanted by another and at the beginning and conclusion of a movement. The motives initially derived from the set are developed, imitated, freely combined with other derived elements, and recapitulated. In short, they behave like motives,[4] even where this behavior requires certain revisions in the ordering of the ever-present set.[5]

Each of the first four movements of the work employs the set in a single aspect, respectively P-0, I-0, R-0, and RI-10 (ex. 88). An analysis of some of the motivic relationships found in the opening section of the first movement is given in example 89. (In ex. 89 the capital letters within brackets call attention to recurrent patterns in rhythm and contour.) Individual notes of the set are occasionally anticipated, the "skipped" elements being stated immediately thereafter, so that no notes of the set are omitted.

---

[3]Ernst Krenek, "New Developments of the Twelve-Tone Technique," *Music Review*, IV (1943), 81 ff.

[4]*Idem, Studies in Counterpoint* (New York, 1940), Chap. II.

[5]Ibid., pp. 3 f. and Chap. VIII.

EXAMPLE 88

EXAMPLE 89

Krenek, Op. 84

Copyright 1942 by G. Schirmer, Inc., New York.
Used by permission.

EXAMPLE 90

The section of the second movement quoted in example 90 illustrates other momentary revisions of the precompositional ordering—the repetition of a note or segment after the appearance of one or several of its successors in the set and the reversed statement of a segment immediately after its "normal" presentation (cf. exx. 90 and 88, *b*).

An unusual device is employed at the conclusion of the third movement. The concluding note of the penultimate statement of the set is omitted, so that the eventual appearance of this note at the conclusion of the final statement of the set also serves to complete the preceding statement. The final note is thereby given, presumably, a certain special emphasis that enhances its cadential function at this point. Such a procedure, of course, must somehow be prepared by preceding musical events. In this connection it is interesting to note that this is the only movement that employs a direct thematic statement of the complete set.

In example 91, from the fourth movement, motives derived from two dovetailed statements of the set are employed antiphonally. The interpolation of successive notes of the set between repetitions of earlier notes is more freely employed in this than in the previous movements (cf. exx. 91 and 88, *d*). This device is merely a variant of one that has been practiced generally in twelve-tone composition, the sustaining of a note while its successors in the set proceed in their regular order, and results in adjacencies that are not directly given in the precompositional linear structure of the set (see Chap. V., secs. I and II).

EXAMPLE 91

Successive segments of each of the four aspects of the set alternate with one another in the fifth movement of the *Suite*. The disposition of the motivic figures in bars 1-5 (ex. 92) is based upon the reciprocal relations of the set-forms: the first pair of pitch elements is inverted in the second pair, the third in the fourth, and so on. In addition, a principle of progression operates in these opening bars that is not directly implied by the set—the gradual reduction of the intervals, from the "major third" to the "minor second." Independent criteria of this sort play a prominent role in securing musical coherence where the compositional elements are so remotely derived from the set that its function as an organizing principle is eliminated or weakened.

EXAMPLE 92

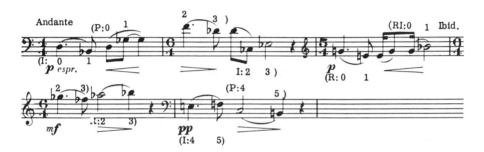

Indeed, in this movement, and in many other works in which the set is conceived as the repository of thematic ideas whose compositional employment need not reveal the original ordering, the set is no longer recognizable as a serial structure. It would seem to be more relevant to analyze such works according to principles of the sort that have been discussed in Chapter II, rather than to offer in lieu of analysis a set traced from indirectly derived sonic details that function more or less independently of it.[6]

Varied linear formations may be extracted from a single form of the set without essential modifications of the original ordering by the employment of the melodically extraneous notes in the "background." This is, in fact, the usual method of deriving such formations. A single illustration is given here (ex. 93). (This procedure, of course, is hardly feasible in a mainly monophonic composition such as Krenek's *Suite for Violoncello Solo*.)

Since the notes of the set are not in principle functionally differentiated, and since there is no all-embracing principle of harmonic propriety as in tonal music, there are no a priori criteria to govern the manner in which "theme" and "accompaniment" are to be derived from the set, a problem which will be dealt with in Chapter V. The number of different linear successions that may be contrived through the retirement of some notes of the set into the "background" is practically unlimited. Such a procedure can be justified, therefore,

---

[6]Cf. Perle, "Theory and Practice in Twelve-Tone Music," *The Score,* June, 1959, 58 ff.

EXAMPLE 93

only where certain restrictions control the derivation of these elements and their compositional employment. Some considerations relevant to this problem have already been presented. They will be treated in greater detail in due course.

III. SEGMENTATION

Informal segmentation procedures have been briefly discussed above, in connection with the Krenek *Suite*. In this section we consider the systematic partitioning of the set into segments, a procedure that permits a great variety of linear elements to be derived from the set without a concomitant weakening of its integrative function.

EXAMPLE 94

Examples 94–96 illustrate the partitioning of the set into segments that internally maintain the original order of their components but that are employed with more or less freedom in relation to one another, as semi-independent subsets. In example 94 the set is divided into two six-note segments that are employed simultaneously. Example 95 is based upon a five-note and a seven-note segment. A great variety of partitionings is found in Schoenberg's *Third Quartet*, Opus 30. In the first movement, for example, the set is systematically trisected into segments of five, two, and five notes, respectively (ex. 96).

EXAMPLE 95

EXAMPLE 96

[cont'd on p. 70]

EXAMPLE 96 [cont'd]

c.

Of more significance than the number and variety of linear formations that may be directly derived from the set through the use of segmentation procedures is the fact that such procedures suggest a special type of set-structure whose transformations and transpositions may be interrelated through segments of common pitch-class content. This concept played a primary role in Schoenberg's work after 1928.

The forty-eight set-forms that may be generated from the set of the third number of Schoenberg's *Three Songs*, Opus 48, for example, are equivalent in terms of hexachordal content, since the two hexachords of the set are, respectively, permutations of the two whole-tone collections. The only members of the set-complex employed in this brief movement are P-0, I-5, and their respective retrograde forms. (Since R-0 and RI-5 may be deduced by simply reading P-0 and I-5 in reverse order, only the two latter forms are illustrated in ex. 97.)

Invariant segmental content is a means of delimiting the range of variational procedures and therefore of maintaining the integrity of the set as an organizing principle in spite of linear revisions. In example 98, from the work cited in the preceding paragraph, linear elements are found that are entirely independent of the set in the ordering of their components, but that nevertheless are derived from the set in terms of their content. An exception

EXAMPLE 97

to the general "rule" prohibiting the omission of notes in any compositional statement of the set (see postulate 1, p. 2) is illustrated in the incomplete statement of P-0 in example 98. The omission is justified by the fact that the content of the unordered segment is implied in this instance by a statement of part of the set.

EXAMPLE 98

The set upon which Opus 48, No. 3, is based is exceptional in that invariance of segmental content is retained under *all* precompositional operations. The typical Schoenbergian set, such as that of the *String Trio*, Opus 45, exhibits this property only within subgroups of the total complex of set-forms (ex. 99).

EXAMPLE 99

IV. THE ASSOCIATION OF "INDEPENDENT" SETS

Revised orderings of the set illustrated in example 99 are systematically employed by Schoenberg in the *String Trio*. In the section entitled "1st Episode" the second half of the set is reordered, and in the "2d Episode" two "new" sets, permuting the internal ordering of both of the original segments, are introduced (ex. 100). These reordered formations represent a modification of the traditional twelve-tone precept that only one set should be used in a composition (see p. 2): on the basis of my earlier definition of the Schoenbergian set as a *specific* permutation of the twelve notes, it is evident that several independent sets appear in this work. In respect to their segmental content, however, all of these are seen to be variants of a single precompositional formation.

EXAMPLE 100

Where the set is defined *exclusively* in terms of its segmental content, as in Hauer's tropes, it may be freely permuted so long as the segmental content is not revised. One of Schoenberg's late works, the *Ode to Napoleon*, discussed in the next chapter (see ex. 132), is based on such a set.

The *Lyric Suite* presents a number of independent sets, related in various ways to the basic set of the first movement (ex. 101, *a*). In the auxiliary sets that appear in the first movement (ex. 101, *b* and *c*), Berg retains the segmental content that the basic set exhibits as a bisected structure. (In other respects invariance of hexachordal content does not play a primary role, as it does in the works of Schoenberg discussed above.) A mere interchange of order numbers 3 and 9 of example 101, *a*, generates the set of the third movement (ex. 102). The sixth movement is based upon the simultaneous use of two sets that are, as abstract precompositional formations, unrelated to each other. In their employment as thematic elements, however, one of these sets is derived from the other: the lower notes (with the exception of order no. 9) of the initial

EXAMPLE 101

EXAMPLE 102

EXAMPLE 103

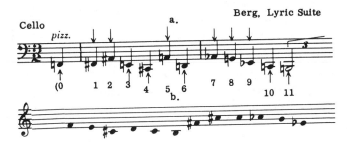

compositional presentation of the first set (ex. 103, *a*)—order numbers 0, 3, 4, 6, 10, and 11—are stated in direct succession as the first half of the second set (ex. 103, *b*), and the remaining notes of the first set in direct succession as the second half of the second set. This derivation is explicitly disclosed in the first- and second-violin parts of bar 30 (ex. 104), which are together equivalent to the inverted first set and individually equivalent to the two six-note segments of the inverted second set. The sixth movement is related to preceding movements through the initial four-note segments of the sets illustrated in examples 101, *a*, and 102, which are incorporated into the set with which the sixth movement commences (ex. 103, *a*). Order numbers 0–3 of example 103, *a*, are identical with the inversion of order numbers 0–3 of example 102, and order numbers 7–10 are identical with order numbers 0–3 (at T–3) of example 101, *a*.

EXAMPLE 104

The opera *Lulu* employs a large number of sets, all derived, according to the composer, from a single basic series (ex. 105, *a*) by means of certain nonaxiomatic precompositional operations.[7] However, several of the ostensible methods of derivation can easily be shown to be specious; they indicate that Berg simply desired to supply some verbal evidence of his adherence to Schoenberg's principle that one should not "use more than one series" (see p. 2).[8]   One of the auxiliary sets, for example, is precompositionally "derived" by (1) presenting in direct succession every fifth note of a circular statement of the basic series; (2) extracting two non-adjacent notes from the set thus

EXAMPLE 105

[7]See Willi Reich, "Alban Berg's *Lulu*," *Musical Quarterly,* XXII (1936), 383 ff.; Reich *et al.,* *Alban Berg* (Vienna: Herbert Reichner Verlag, 1937), pp. 112 f.; Reich, *Alban Berg* (London: Thames and Hudson, 1965), pp. 161 ff. René Leibowitz, Humphrey Searle, and others recapitulate the analysis by Reich, which is based on a private communication from the composer.

[8]See Hans Keller, "Lulu," *Music Review,* XIV (1953), 302 f.

generated and presenting them together as a vertical formation; (3) cyclically permuting the remaining notes; (4) partitioning this cyclical permutation into two five-note segments; (5) freely reordering the content of each segment.[9] The formation supposedly derived in this way (ex. 105, *c*) may be far less laboriously derived from any one of numerous sets other than the one that is supposed to be its source—for example, the principal set of the first movement of the *Lyric Suite* (ex. 106):

EXAMPLE 106

Moreover, the very first step of the extraordinary procedure described above is rendered superfluous by the derivation of another one of the auxiliary sets employed in *Lulu* from every seventh note of the basic series, of which a derived set consisting of every fifth note is merely the retrograde (cyclically permuted so that the order numbers are 11, 0, 1, . . . 10).

The compositional relationships musically unfolded, however, reveal a logic, architectonic skill, and imagination that are of the first order.[10] The wealth of thematic material evolved through the association of numerous independent twelve-tone sets of various types is employed with the greatest freedom without disrupting the organizing function of the sets themselves. The latter may be classified as follows: (1) linearly ordered sets, or "series"; (2) sets partitioned into two or more mutually exclusive segments of unordered content, comparable to Hauer's tropes though not necessarily hexachordal in structure (ex. 105, *c*); (3) "serial tropes," that is, sets partitioned into internally ordered segments that are subjected, independently of the set as a whole, to such serial operations as will not revise the relative content of the respective segments (ex. 107); (4) "harmonic tropes," that is, sets partitioned into segments of an essentially chordal, rather than linear, character (ex. 108).

EXAMPLE 107

X(p-o)   Y(p-o)   Z(p-o)

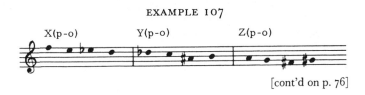

[cont'd on p. 76]

---

[9]In other words, each segment is ultimately defined as an unordered collection in the set thus "derived." The original serial ordering is employed on occasion, however.

[10]See Perle, "*Lulu:* Thematic Material and Pitch Organization," *Music Review*, XXII (1965), 269 ff.

EXAMPLE 107 [cont'd]

EXAMPLE 108

Berg's twelve-tone practice must be distinguished from Schoenberg's not only because of his indifference to Schoenberg's principle that one should not "use more than one series" and his employment of nonserial sets, but also because even in his exploitation of an individual series, or "tone row," his practice is radically different from Schoenberg's in several fundamental respects:

(1) Specific linear contours characterize the serial sets, contours that are employed referentially in a manner that has no analogue in the thematic set statements of Schoenberg's *Fourth Quartet* or *Concerto for Piano and Orchestra* (cf. p. 61). In some instances this contour is assumed to retain its identity when it is inverted but never when it is reversed. Thus the retrograde and retrograde-inversion—aspects of the series that are less likely to be melodically identifiable with the prime—are almost never employed except as components of a palindrome that embraces the whole musical texture, as in the sextet of Act I, Scene 3, of *Lulu*, or in the interlude between the two scenes of Act II. Berg's serial procedures in his other twelve-tone works also conform to this principle. Only in the first movement of the *Lyric Suite*, for example, are R and RI set-forms regularly found that are not part of a palindrome; but the set of that movement (ex. 101, *a*) is a symmetrical series that has no

independent R and RI forms, these being respectively equivalent to tritone transpositions of the prime and inversion. (Segments of serial tropes in *Lulu* are regularly employed in their retrograde aspects, as in example 107; but these segments are sufficiently limited in extent, so that the referential contour is clear regardless of its direction.) The extent to which a specific contour is associated with the ordered sets of *Lulu* is implied in the fact that in its derivation from the basic series (ex. 109, *a*) the serial trope illustrated in example 109, *b*, preserves in its characteristic melodic contour each element at the relative register in which that element occurs within a referential melodic contour of the basic series.

EXAMPLE 109

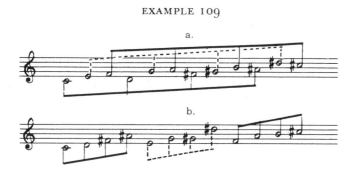

(2) Whereas in Schoenberg's twelve-tone practice a motive that is compositionally extracted from the series remains a component of a total twelve-tone texture wherever it recurs, in *Lulu* such motives are often used independently of their original or any other connection with the set. The melodic pattern illustrated in ex. 110, for instance, is originally extracted (Act I, bars 258-259) from the inverted basic series. In subsequent appearances it is often more remotely related to the series and sometimes not related at all.

EXAMPLE 110

Berg, Lulu, Act I, bars 258–259.

(3) While certain harmonic formations in *Lulu* are serially derived, the texture in general is not dependent on serial procedures but on the assumption of a pervasive harmonic atmosphere based on the preferential employment of certain sonorities, a harmonic background that exists prior to any given series just as the triadic texture of traditional tonality exists prior to any given melodic detail. With Schoenberg and Webern it is the set that presumably determines the harmonic texture, but in *Lulu* a large number of different sets are integrated by virtue of their common dependence on a given harmonic background. It is not easy to describe this background, which comprises diatonic, chromatic, and dodecaphonic elements. How little it has in common with whatever one may understand by the "twelve-tone system" is suggested in many places by the lowermost part, whose notes are frequently chosen not because of any serial considerations but for the sake of harmonic movement and direction. For example, the bass line often progresses chromatically in long note values. Certainly it would be specious to describe such progressions as more or less "freely derived" from segments of Schigolch's set (ex. 107). On the contrary, this set is itself chosen because its presence as an important melodic structure invests *any* chromatic progression with a somewhat thematic character. Other bass progressions comprise segments of whole-tone or diatonic scales that may similarly be identified with, but not "derived" from, Lulu's set (ex. 84). Characteristic harmonic procedures of the "strict" twelve-tone system, in particular the vertical statement of segments of the set, play an important role in *Lulu*, but they do not, as with Schoenberg and Webern, determine the overall harmonic texture. They are simply some, among many, components of this texture.[11]

V. THE INCORPORATION OF NONDODECAPHONIC ELEMENTS INTO THE SET

Idiomatic details that are characteristic of other musical systems are sometimes introduced into a twelve-tone work, either as deliberately extraneous elements or as integral features of the total material. Nondodecaphonic linear formations are easily contrived from a twelve-tone set by means of some of the devices discussed earlier in this chapter, particularly that of retiring the melodically extraneous notes into the "background" (see pp. 67 f.). The set may be specially constructed to incorporate features not normally associated with the twelve-tone system. A well-known example is the set of Berg's *Violin Concerto* (ex. 126), whose overlapping segments comprise statements of each of the triadic formations of the major-minor system and part of the whole-tone scale. Other examples are discussed in section III of Chapter V.

---

[11]This paragraph is taken from my article, "The Music of *Lulu:* A New Analysis," *Journal of the American Musicological Society*, XII (1959), 189. Cf. n. 23, Chap. VI.

VI. FUNCTION OF THE BASIC CELL
IN TWELVE-TONE MUSIC

The twelve-tone set may be regarded as an expansion of the basic cell, which, as we have seen, performed an important integrative function in "free" atonality. In many of the later works of Webern the set itself is a composite structure generated by the literal transformations of a component serial unit. The *Concerto for Nine Instruments*, Opus 24, for example, is based on the set shown in example 111. The set (at P-0) is seen to comprise the following statements of a three-note subset: p-0, ri-7, r-6, i-1. (The lower-case letters represent the four aspects of the subset.) Every compositional element is thus ultimately derived from a single microcosmic detail, and the operations of that detail are preestablished in a higher structural entity, the set. The common segmental content of different forms of this set suggests a means of association and differentiation at a still higher compositional level. The following set-forms, for instance, are permutations and internal reorderings of the four segments of example 111: P-0, I-1, P-6, I-7, and their retrograde versions. The compositional implications of these relationships are only occasionally realized in this work, as in the opening of the first movement (ex. 112).

EXAMPLE 111

EXAMPLE 112

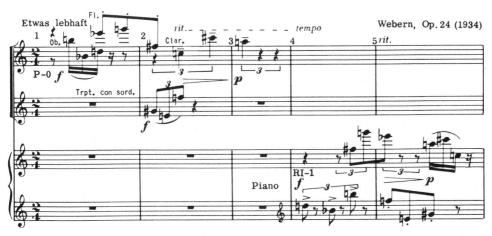

P-0 and RI-1 are linearly unfolded here, resulting in the following succession of subsets: p-0, ri-7, r-6, i-1 / r-0, i-7, p-6, ri-1. The pitch content of each subset of P-0 is duplicated in the subset that occupies the same relative position in RI-1, but with the internal ordering of this content reversed. At the same time, the first half of P-0 is literally transposed in the second half of RI-1, and the second half of P-0 is literally transposed in the first half of RI-1.

As in the "free" atonal works of Webern, dynamics, rhythm, timbre, and the specific octave position of the individual pitches are employed structurally (see pp. 18 f. and 21 ff.). A "thematic" rhythmic formation coincides with the initial statement of the set and, like that statement, consists of phases of a single three-note figure. This rhythmic "set"—presented in bars 1-3, 4-5, 45-47, 63-64, and 65-67—is generated by the application of different degrees of augmentation to the initial sixteenth-note subset. Rhythmically the first two statements of the set are related as "prime" to "retrograde," dynamically as "prime" to "prime." The invariance of segmental content in these initial statements of P-0 and RI-1 is compositionally emphasized by the retention of the orginal octave position of each note. The primary structural entities are also differentiated with regard to timbre: the first statement of the set is given to the winds, with each segment presented in a different instrument; the second statement is given to the piano.

Even where the set is not derived from a single cell, its compositional employment in Webern's works is almost always based upon minimal motivic relationships, as in the *Quartet*, Opus 22, for violin, clarinet, tenor saxophone, and piano. In the opening bars (ex. 113) the prime and inversion unfold simultaneously in corresponding segments of 3, 3, 2, 1, and 3 notes.

EXAMPLE 113

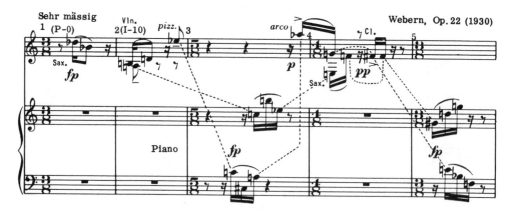

The following quotation from the second movement (bars 19 ff.) demonstrates the fantastic density and variety of polyphonic relationships that unfold in a texture of only two parts (ex. 114).

EXAMPLE II4[12]

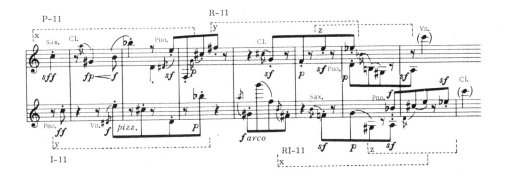

The passage as a whole is a canon by inversion of pitch-class order and contour; brackets x and y enclose rhythmic patterns interchanged between the two parts; brackets z enclose a canonic fragment that maintains the imitative principle in respect to pitch-class order, contour, rhythm, mode of attack, and timbre. At the same time, in opposition to the inversional pitch relations generated by the paired set-forms, there is an interplay of invariant two-note segments, projected by means of register, mode of attack, and rhythm. Through various types of segmentation an extraordinary variety of associations are established among the different set-forms throughout the work. In the second movement, for example, several episodes are based on recurrent figures generated by an ingenious partitioning of paired set-forms related to each other as P-0 is to RI-7 (ex. 115).

EXAMPLE II5

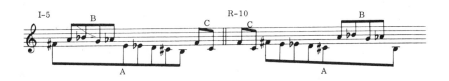

---

[12]The comments on exs. 114 and 115 and the further discussion of Opus 22 in Chap. VI are taken from my article, "Webern's Twelve-Tone Sketches," *The Musical Quarterly*, LVII (1971).

Such traditional concepts as "theme" and "background" usually have no place in the works of Webern. The compositional events unfold in terms of expanded serial relations that govern not only melodic and harmonic elements but also, to a certain extent, dynamic details, rhythms, timbres, and the specific octave positions of the notes. Such minor revisions of the precompositionally established ordering of the notes as are normally found even in the so-called "strict" twelve-tone compositions of other composers do not occur.

The derivation of a set from a single cell as in Webern's *Concerto for Nine Instruments* is a method regularly employed in the works of Milton Babbitt in order to generate auxiliary, or, as he terms them, "derived," sets from a single fundamental set.[13] The basic set of Babbitt's *Composition for Four Instruments,* explicitly stated only at the conclusion of the work, is shown in ex. 116:

EXAMPLE 116

This set is partitioned into four three-note segments, as indicated in the example. Each segment of any form of the basic set may function as the generating unit of a derived set (see ex. 117).

EXAMPLE 117

The generating unit may also be a four-note or a six-note segment of a basic set. The initial four-note segment and either six-note segment of example 118, *a*, for instance, may generate derived sets (see ex. 118, *b*).

[13]See Babbitt, "Some Aspects of Twelve-Tone Composition," *The Score and I.M.A. Magazine,* June 1955, pp. 59 f.; and Babbitt's review of Leibowitz, *Schoenberg et son école* and *Qu'est-ce que la musique de douze sons?* In *Journal of the American Musicological Society,* III (1950), 60.

EXAMPLE 118

In the *Allegro misterioso* of the *Lyric Suite* two durational patterns derived from the characteristic registral distribution of the elements of the set (ex. 119, *a*) function as basic rhythmic cells. At the first entrance of the cello (ex. 119, *b*) these rhythmic cells, in augmentation, are imposed upon the characteristic permutations of the basic four-note pitch cell (cf. ex. 87).

EXAMPLE 119

It hardly needs to be emphasized that linear elements in twelve-tone music, as in tonal music, cannot be adequately discussed apart from other components. The derivation of a twelve-tone set by means of serial operations upon a segment of that set, as in examples 111, 117, and 118, presuppose types of set-structure that have a special relevance to the subject matter of the following chapters. At the same time, further elucidation of the linear aspects of twelve-tone music requires consideration of its formal and vertical aspects.

V
Simultaneity

I. THE VERTICALIZATION OF ADJACENCIES[1]

In the examples from Debussy, Roslavetz, and Scriabin discussed in Chapter III, the set — consisting of notes *selected* out of the possible twelve — is employed not only as the basis of linear association but even more consistently as the basis of vertical association. Since in these instances the set is not ordered, the concept of adjacency does not appear, but only that of content. The total content of the set is here the sole general criterion of harmonic propriety. The Schoenbergian set, however, comprises *all* the notes of the chromatic scale; its total content, therefore, cannot serve as a means of delimiting harmonic possibilities. Instead, the precompositional linear ordering is realized vertically through the employment of successive groups of contiguous notes of the set as chords.

But this device is only one basis of simultaneity. The verticalization of linearly ordered elements imposes certain compositional restrictions that quite preclude its exclusive determination of harmonic relations. And even verticalization, the only harmonic procedure ostensibly consistent with the premise of linear ordering, does not unambiguously represent this ordering.

In both diatonic tonality and the twelve-tone system a precompositional harmonic criterion is assumed: in the former this is the triad; in the latter it is adjacency of the elements in the set. Every tonal combination is either itself a triad or a component of a progression whose origin and destination are triads. In twelve-tone music, however, simultaneity may or may not conform to the only ordering principle provided by the system, and where it does not do so it bears no necessary relation to this principle.

The beginning of Schoenberg's *Fourth Quartet* is a relatively simple illustration of verticalization. In the excerpt quoted below the inverted set is linearly stated and at the same time segmented into four three-note vertical

---

[1]Several excerpts from my article "The Harmonic Problem in Twelve-Tone Music," *Music Review*, XV (1954), 253 ff., are incorporated, in revised and expanded form, in sections I, II, III, and VI of this chapter, with the kind permission of the editor of that publication.

formations. The vertical adjacencies, however, do not necessarily conform to the horizontal adjacencies. At v and y the chords do so conform but the vertical adjacencies into which the other chords may be analyzed do not correspond to the linear arrangement.

EXAMPLE 120

Schoenberg, Op. 37

The following statement can be made concerning twelve-tone harmonic practice as revealed in this and almost all other twelve-tone compositions: when linearly adjacent elements are simultaneously stated, the original ordering may be disregarded so long as the harmonic entity is identical in content with a segment of the set. The harmonic relevance of the linear formation is thus in inverse proportion to the number of elements that constitute this segment. Obviously, if the harmonic formation contains only two notes the vertical and the horizontal adjacencies will be identical. And if it contains twelve notes it will have no relation to a unique linear arrangement since it could function as a verticalization of any set.

Further consideration of example 120 discloses another problematical aspect of twelve-tone harmony. As in triadic music, there is a melody and its chordal accompaniment. It is important, however, to distinguish between the two systems with respect to the manner in which the two planes are interrelated. In triadic music each melodic element has an unambiguous relationship to the chord that serves as its background. Such a relationship does not exist in example 120. At v the melodic note might be interpreted as a "chordal" element since it is contiguous in the set to the three-note segment that is verticalized to accompany it. At w and y the melodic notes are "nonchordal" from this point of view. The melodic note, at w and at y, anticipates an element of the subsequent vertical formation. At z the $b\flat$ in the melody operates in a double capacity: as the final element of the linear statement of the set and as a member of the final verticalized segment. But these various distinctions have no clear function in a system that has no a priori harmonic standard of reference, such as the triad.

The absence of an explicit harmonic interrelation between the horizontal and the vertical plane does not necessarily invalidate the method of chord construction under discussion. The melodic elements are heard in a distinct dimension and do not obscure the verticalized segments that form the harmonic background. Yet there are a good many instances in twelve-tone music of simultaneities that do not reveal the distinction between adjacent and nonadjacent elements presupposed by the employment of the set. In example 121 (from the first movement of Webern's *Variations* for piano) the context and structure of the harmonic element d-$g\sharp$-$f\sharp$ conceal the fact that the d and $f\sharp$ are a verticalized adjacency and the $g\sharp$ is a linearly stated member of another aspect of the set.

But even where harmonic elements are limited to verticalized segments of a single set-form, the linear ordering is in general observed only in part, as was pointed out above. An exceptional attempt to represent the original linear ordering in verticalized segments of the set is found in the first of Babbitt's *Three Compositions for Piano.* Simultaneities here either maintain the linear adjacencies (ex. 122), as in the Schoenberg example (120) at v and y, or else progressively set forth the original ordering (ex. 123).

EXAMPLE 121

EXAMPLE 122

EXAMPLE 123

II. THE VERTICALIZATION OF NONADJACENT LINEAR ELEMENTS

The melodic revision of the preestablished linear relations through the delayed repetition of a note or segment of the set has been discussed in the preceding chapter (section II). An analogous procedure, the repeating or sustaining of one or more notes of the set while the remainder of the set unfolds in its normal order, is a generally accepted means of deriving harmonic elements that do not conform to the adjacency criterion. The resulting formations often are not in any way implied by the structure of the set. The repetitions in example 124, for instance, are obviously motivated by the desire to arrive at a special sonority for cadential purposes, a sonority based on an interval that is not an element of the set.

Certain compositional attitudes must be formulated in response to the practical problems that arise as a result of the employment of independent formations of this sort in a twelve-tone work. It would seem, for example, that simultaneities conforming to the adjacency axiom ought somehow to be aurally distinguishable from those that do not so conform, since otherwise it

EXAMPLE 124

would seem to be impossible to justify verticalization as a harmonic procedure. As a sort of corollary to this requirement the possibility suggests itself, where nonadjacent notes are vertically associated, of deploying every dynamic, motivic, and rhythmic means to fortify the harmonic moment against independent harmonic meaning. Another approach would be the regulation of harmonic detail by some consistent principle, independent or semi-independent of the ordering of the elements in the set. A principle of this sort, illustrated in the next section, is the assumption of some pervasive harmonic texture based on the preferential employment of certain intervals. These considerations concern the mind and ear of both composer and listener in a real, practical sense; they are verified as fully by the musical deficiencies that follow from their insufficient realization as by the positive results that depend upon their observance.

In many of the works of Webern the structure of the set itself results in a certain consistency of harmonic texture that establishes a criterion for the harmonic association of nonadjacent elements. An example is the set of Opus 24 (ex. 111), with its preponderance of "major thirds" and "minor seconds" among adjacent elements.

III. THE INCORPORATION OF TONAL ELEMENTS INTO THE SET

As I have shown, criteria not necessarily dependent upon the structure of the set often play an important role in determining harmonic relations. O. W. Neighbour, dealing with this problem in his article "In Defense of Schönberg," suggests that Schoenberg's harmony "is an extension of post-Wagnerian chromatic writing, but that the development of its ellipses and ambiguities has led to such a wide range of situations that it is more bewildering at first encounter than some other systems" and that there "is some kind of tonality present."[2]   It is observable that one of the basic attitudes mentioned above, the regulation of harmonic detail by some consistent principle more or less independent of the set, operates in example 120. There, a certain harmonic interval, the "minor sixth," is employed in preference to others, although it still does not function as a standard of harmonic reference, as does the triad in tonal music. The four three-note segments of the set can each be stated in six different arrangements, among which adjacent elements at the interval of a "minor sixth" will be present as follows: in two verticalizations of the first segment, in none of the second segment, in three of the third segment, and in two of the fourth segment. The appearance of this interval among adjacent elements in each simultaneity in the example except that at x, where it is precluded by the set-structure, would seem to be the result of a definite criterion of selection rather than a consequence of either set-structure or chance. That such a criterion should be interpreted in terms of the harmonic relations of tonality, as Mr. Neighbour assumes of Schoenberg's twelve-tone harmony in general, seems to me highly doubtful.

The harmonic practice of Alban Berg, however, frequently invites such interpretation. In *Der Wein* and the *Violin Concerto* the structure of the set itself suggests characteristic features of diatonic tonality (exx. 125 and 126). In both of these works definite tonal ends dictate the specific dodecaphonic procedures.

In *Lulu* and the *Lyric Suite*, where no such primary purpose operates, tonal relationships still play an important role. The harmonic texture includes diatonic, chromatic, and dodecaphonic elements, integrated into "some kind

EXAMPLE 125

---

[2]In *Music and Letters*, XXXIII (1952), 10 ff. See also O. W. Neighbour, "A Talk on Schoenberg," *The Score and I.M.A. Magazine*, June 1956, 19 ff.

EXAMPLE 126

Berg, Violin Concerto, 1st Movement

EXAMPLE 127

of tonality." In example 127, the basic set of the first movement of the *Lyric Suite*, segments that are vertically statable as triads or seventh chords are indicated by brackets. Tonal relationships are suggested even where the harmonic detail is not an immediately identifiable traditional formation. Consistent with this approach is the special treatment accorded the interval of the perfect fifth in the first movement. Each half of the set is permutable into a series of perfect fifths, the auxiliary set thus formed (ex. 101, *b*) being employed in a secondary capacity as the source of certain harmonic and melodic occurrences. It is stated in vertical segments, for instance, as an introduction, even before the initial appearance of the basic set (ex. 127), and is stated linearly in its retrograde aspect in the cello part at bars 7-9. The elementary structure of the auxiliary set results in the immediate aural recognition of relationships between linear and harmonic elements derived therefrom, but these relationships are of such salient and limited character as to render this set useful for only a minimum of compositional purposes. The tonal associations of these and of other details provide a basis for harmonic reference, a relatively ambiguous one, to be sure, but resulting to a limited extent in functional differentiation and even harmonic direction.

The preponderance of particular intervals in the structure of the set automatically assures a certain textural homogeneity. Should the structure of the set at the same time suggest characteristic features of a familiar musical idiom, as in the *Violin Concerto*, explicit criteria, independent of the twelve-tone system, may affect the harmonic activity of the set. Modifications of the preestablished linear ordering may be motivated largely by the desire to achieve certain musical effects traditionally associated with the major-minor system. No general solution is to be found here for the special problems with which this chapter is concerned. Harmonic relations in twelve-tone music cannot in general thus depend upon a borrowed harmonic language, based upon premises that have no general meaning in the twelve-tone system.

Traditional triadic elements play an important role in Schoenberg's *Ode to Napoleon*. This work will be discussed in a later section of this chapter, since both the structure of the set and the manner in which it is employed require certain special considerations.

IV. INVARIANT FORMATIONS

The association of set-forms through segments of common content has been referred to frequently in earlier chapters. Such invariant elements are particularly useful as a means of reducing and simplifying the harmonic formulations generated by the verticalization of set-segments. An extreme instance is illustrated in example 128, from the second movement of the *Symphony*, Opus 21, by Webern. The reiterated chords may be interpreted as verticalized segments of any one of the following set-forms: P–11, R–11 (equivalent to P–5), I–2, or RI–2 (equivalent to I–8). That each of these in turn is the source of the harmonic pattern is revealed only in the linear ordering of the four-note segment given to the harp.

EXAMPLE 128

Webern, Op. 21

[cont'd on p. 92]

EXAMPLE 128 [cont'd]

Webern's *II. Kantate*, Opus 31, is based upon a set whose corresponding P-0 and I-0 six-note segments have five notes in common (ex. 129). Coherent harmonic relationships are achieved in the first movement of this work through the employment of these segments (ex. 130).

EXAMPLE 129

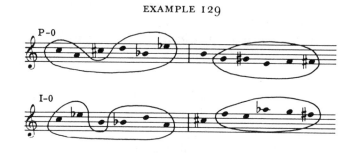

EXAMPLE 130

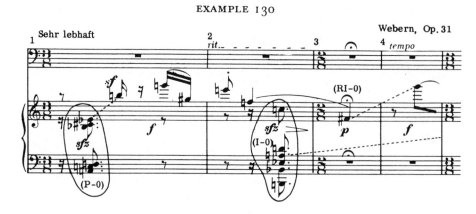

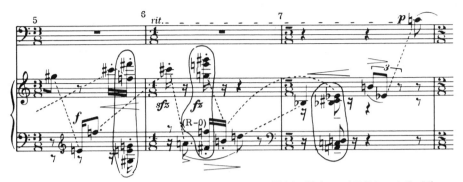

The initial six-note segments of six different forms of a set are associated through a common harmonic element in Schoenberg's *A Survivor from Warsaw* (ex. 131):

EXAMPLE 131

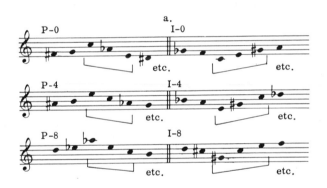

V. SEGMENTATION

We have seen that chords derived through the verticalization of linear relationships disregard to a certain extent the original ordering of the set, the set being considered, for harmonic purposes, as a collection of segments of specified but unordered content. Possibly as a concomitant of the resultant weakening of the linearly premised order, many of the melodic details are also derived from freely linearized segments of the set (see pp. 70-71). In the *String Trio* by Schoenberg, discussed in the preceding chapter, several different sets may be deduced, each of these being merely another linear permutation of the same basic six-note segments.

The *Ode to Napoleon*, Opus 41, implies no precompositional linear ordering whatever, the set being definable exclusively in terms of its hexachordal content. Moreover, since the two hexachords are freely interchanged and since each may be inverted without revision of its content, the third of the postulates of set-structure (p. 2), which affirms that the set may be stated in any of its linear aspects, has no meaning. The precompositional material is further limited by the fact that the special structure of the set permits any member of the set-complex to be restated on any degree of the whole-tone scale without alteration of the content of its two segments, so that it is possible to obtain only two nonequivalent set-forms and four nonequivalent segments (ex. 132: A, B, C, D). A variety of harmonic elements, including the traditional triads, are derived from these segments (ex. 133).

EXAMPLE 132

In some respects the serial procedures employed in the *Ode* are reminiscent of one of Schoenberg's earliest essays in twelve-tone composition, the middle section and other sections of the "Tanzscene" from the *Serenade*, Opus 24 (bars 56-111, 128-133, 177-184, 199-200). Here, too, a bisected set (ex. 134) is employed, in which the order of the notes is freely permuted within the segment. Since the content of the second segment is the inversion, at T–5 or T–11, of the content of the first, inversion of the set at either pitch level does not revise the content of the segments but merely interchanges the two hexachords.

Example 135 is an extract from this work, illustrating the derivation of melodic elements from one hexachord, harmonic elements from the other.

EXAMPLE 133

Schoenberg, Op. 41

EXAMPLE 134

EXAMPLE 135

Schoenberg, Op. 24

Transpositions at the tritone merely reorder the original content of the segments (cf. bar 177 with 179, and 178 with 180). This is the earliest instance of one of Schoenberg's most common methods of differentiating melodic from harmonic material—the assignment of distinct segments of the set to each component.

Among the numerous examples of this procedure as applied to an ordered set is *Sommermüd*, No. 1 of *Three Songs*, Opus 48. In the opening bars

EXAMPLE 136

Schoenberg, Op. 48, No. 1 (1933)

Wenn du schon glaubst,____ es ist e - wi - ge Nacht,____

(ex. 136) the linear ordering is respected only in the vocal part, with the four-note segment that is given to the piano defined only in terms of its content.

The invariant segmental content of the set on which the third song of this group is based was illustrated in the preceding chapter (exx. 97 and 98). The four hexachords comprised within the set-forms employed in this work—P-0 and R-0, I-5, and RI-5—are bisected to provide a series of three-note units that function as the harmonic material of the piece (ex. 137).

EXAMPLE 137

VI. THE SIMULTANEOUS STATEMENT OF DIFFERENT SET-FORMS

The verticalization of linearly adjacent elements of the set concerns only one—a primarily homophonic—aspect of simultaneity in twelve-tone music. The vertical association of nonadjacent elements is normally the result of a simultaneous statement of two or more of the forty-eight members of the set-complex. Where two or more set-forms are simultaneously employed—a primarily polyphonic procedure—the problem of selection is again complicated by the absence of a precompositional standard of harmonic reference, the function fulfilled by the triad in tonal music. In his essay "Composition with Twelve Tones," Schoenberg, citing as the controlling factor the only restrictive precept of vertical association in twelve-tone music—prohibition of the octave—describes various methods for effecting linear simultaneity. Only one of these methods has Schoenberg consistently employed in his later works. In his own words:

Later, especially in larger works, I changed my original idea, if necessary, to fit the following conditions: the inversion a fifth below of the first six tones, the antecedent, should not produce a repetition of one of these six tones, but should bring forth the hitherto unused six tones of the chromatic scale. Thus, the consequent of the basic set, the tones 7 to 12 [order nos. 6-11], comprises the tones of this inversion, but, of course, in a different order.[3]

This means that the prime set must be so constructed that when it is simultaneously stated with its inversion each half of the prime combines with the corresponding half of the inversion to form an aggregate of the twelve pitch classes of the semitonal scale (see pp. 6 f.). This aggregate is not identical with the precompositional linear ordering, but it is consistent with the primary axioms of set-structure. Having no derivation other than the set, it is a corollary of the horizontal structure of the set.

The procedure that Schoenberg describes limits his aggregate structures to those generated through the vertical alignment of six-note segments of P–0 and I–5, and of correspondingly related set-forms. Directly analogous procedures that he does not describe will permit a similar association of set-forms separated by other intervals, of set-forms of any aspect, of set-forms characterized by other types of segmental structure, and finally, of more than two set-forms. The theoretical implications of Schoenberg's discovery have been developed in the writings of Milton Babbitt,[4] who considers that here is the key to an autonomous twelve-tone music, in which all aspects of the work—form, the constitution and interrelation of linear and vertical details, even rhythm—will be referable to a basic set, just as these elements are referable to the triad in the diatonic tonal system. This principle of set-association has been termed "combinatoriality" by Babbitt, who distinguishes between the "semi-combinatorial" and the "all-combinatorial" set, as follows:

[The semi-combinatorial set] is a set so constructed that *one* of its transformations, other than its retrograde, can be transposed so that its first six notes are equivalent, with regard only to content, to the last six notes of the original set. The first six notes of each of these two sets will then, together, contain all twelve notes. The same condition will hold for the second halves of the sets and, by symmetry, the same relations will hold between the remaining basic forms of the set. The nature of the retrograde

---

[3]Schoenberg, *Style and Idea,* p. 225.

[4]See, in addition to those cited on pp. 2 and 82, above, and n. 5, below, "Set Structure as a Compositional Determinant," *Journal of Music Theory.* V (1961), 72 ff.

operation assures comparable linear properties. This principle can be generalized to the construction of the all-combinatorial set, which possesses such a relation to *all* of its transformations and one, or more, of its own transpositions.[5]

A twelve-tone aggregate is, of course, always present where corresponding six-note segments of P-0 and R-0, or of equivalently related set-forms, are combined. In all other cases a special type of set-structure is required: (1) in order to effect combinatoriality between a prime set-form and an inverted set-form, or between equivalently related set-forms, the content of one half of the set must be the inversion of the content of its other half; (2) in order to effect combinatoriality between two set-forms that are related as prime to retrograde-inversion, the content of each half of the set must be statable as its own inversion; (3) in order to effect combinatoriality between two transpositions of a single set-form, the content of one half of the set must be a transposition of the content of the other half. The all-combinatorial set simultaneously fulfills all three requirements. (The fulfillment of any two of these requirements automatically assures fulfillment of the remaining one.) The combinatorial principle may be similarly applied to the construction of four-note segments to permit the formation of twelve-tone aggregates through the alignment of three sets at a time, and to the construction of three-note segments to permit the construction of twelve-tone aggregates through the alignment of four sets at a time. (See pp. 129 ff.)

EXAMPLE 138

Schoenberg restricts himself to the type of combinatorial relation described in the quotation from his article given at the beginning of this section, based on the association of a prime and an inverted set-form. Example 138 illustrates the principal P and I combinatorial pair of set-forms employed in the *Klavierstück*, Opus 33a. Reciprocal relations among members of the set-complex assure combinatoriality between the following paired sets employed in the course of this work: P-0 and I-5, R-0 and RI-5, P-2 and I-7, P-7 and I-0, R-7 and RI-0.

The *Klavierstück*, Opus 33b, is restricted to a single combinatorial pair and its retrograde statement (ex. 139). In the extract quoted below, each of the two

[5] A review of *Polyphonie, quatrième cahier,* in *Journal of the American Musicological Society,* III (1950), 265.

EXAMPLE 139

EXAMPLE 140

Schoenberg, Op. 33b

phrases consists of a single twelve-tone aggregate, in which the melody is derived from one and the accompaniment from the other of the associated sets.

The concept of set-association based on invariance of segmental content, discussed earlier, is the converse of that of combinatoriality. If the content of a six-note segment of one set-form is identical with the content of a given segment of another set-form, then the one segment will have no elements in common with the remaining segment of the second set-form, and will therefore form a twelve-tone aggregate with this remaining segment. The set of Schoenberg's Opus 48, No. 3 (ex. 97) generates a complex all forty-eight of whose members maintain invariance of segmental content with P-0, either between corresponding or between noncorresponding hexachords, that is, between hexachords that occupy the same relative position in their respective set-forms or between hexachords that do not occupy the same relative position. Any set-form in this case will be combinatorially associable, through the simultaneous statement of hexachords of mutually exclusive content, with any other set-form at *all* transpositional levels.

The properties displayed by the set of Opus 48, No. 3, exceed the minimum requirements for an all-combinatorial set. A set fulfilling, in terms of its segmental content, only these minimum requirements is illustrated below. The

EXAMPLE 141

example presents the various set-forms employed in the first movement of Babbit's *Three Compositions for Piano*. Each set-form in either column may be combinatorially paired, through corresponding segments of mutually exclusive content, with any one of the set-forms in the other column. As in Schoenberg's Opus 33*b*, the original transpositional level of the combinatorial group as a whole — comprising, in this instance, eight non-equivalent set-forms — is retained throughout the movement. Any pair of set-forms in the example that may not be combinatorially associated through corresponding segments may be combinatorially associated through noncorresponding segments. Example 142, *a*, illustrates twelve-tone aggregates based on corresponding segments; example 142, *b*, illustrates twelve-tone aggregates based on noncorresponding segments.

At this point I digress momentarily from the main topic of this chapter in order to present a principle of linear continuity that Babbitt has developed as a concomitant of combinatoriality: the linear association of set-forms through what he terms "secondary sets," that is, successive statements of noncorresponding six-note segments that together form a twelve-tone aggregate.[6] Such a secondary set is formed, for example, by the second segment of P-0 in example 141 and the first segment of P-0, R-6, I-7, or RI-1, when any one of the four latter set-forms is stated immediately after P-0. Linear continuity is effected entirely by means of secondary sets in the excerpts from Babbitt's composition quoted in example 142.

Combinatoriality is the only general principle for the simultaneous alignment of different set-forms that has so far been developed. It has been entirely neglected by Berg and Webern. Its converse, however, set-association based on invariance of segmental content, plays an important role in the works of both

---

[6]Babbitt, "Some Aspects of Twelve-Tone Composition," *The Score and I.M.A. Magazine,* June 1955, pp. 56 f.

EXAMPLE 142

a.

Babbitt, Three Compositions for Piano, No. 1 (1947)

[cont'd on p. 102]

EXAMPLE 142 [cont'd]
b.

composers, as we have seen. In analyzing and evaluating Berg's procedures it is often necessary to resort to empirical analytical methods such as were employed in the chapter on "free" atonal composition. *Lulu* is a remarkable example of a work that integrates the concept of set-association through segmental invariance with features of both "free" atonal and tonal composition.[7]

The tonal orientation of the first movement of Berg's *Lyric Suite* has already been demonstrated. In example 143 the harmonic texture is successively derived from verticalized set-adjacencies and vertically aligned linear state-

EXAMPLE 143

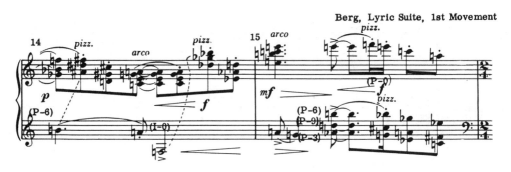

---

[7]See Perle, articles cited in Chapter IV, above, notes 10 and 11, and pp. 135 ff., below.

ments of four different set-forms. The tritones that the basic set (ex. 127) presents between its initial and final notes and between its two central notes together form a "diminished-seventh" chord that remains invariant at its original pitch level in the four forms of the set simultaneously stated (bars 15 ff.). This invariant formation determines the selection of set-forms not only at this point but also in the movement as a whole. Other instances of the use of invariant formations as a basis for set-association have been cited in section IV of this chapter.

The desire for a special type of sonority, employing doublings at the third and sixth, motivates the choice of set-forms in Variation I (bars 58–81) of Schoenberg's *Variations for Orchestra,* Opus 31 (ex. 144).

EXAMPLE 144

Schoenberg, Op. 31

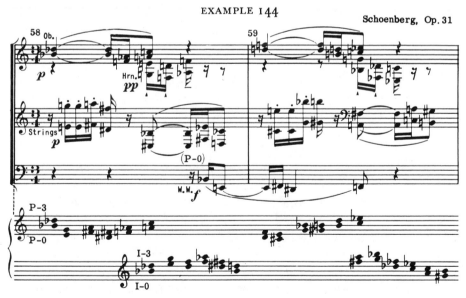

EXAMPLE 145

Webern, Op. 27

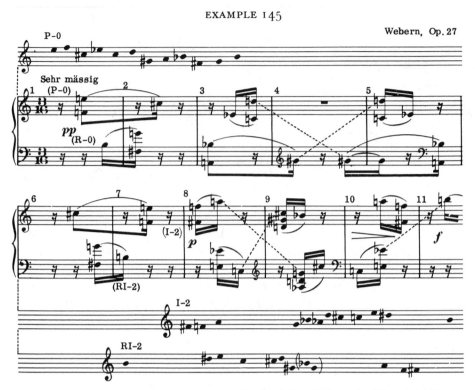

A specific formal plan may provide the basis of set-association. In the first movement of Webern's *Variations* for piano, for instance, each phrase proceeds to a certain point and then (except for some octave transpositions and rhythmic alterations) retraces its steps in reverse order (ex. 145). Each set-form is paired with its retrograde version, the interchange of segments of common content but reversed order determining the formal design.

VII. THE OCTAVE RELATION IN TWELVE-TONE MUSIC

The tendency to avoid the octave in "free" atonal music has been discussed in Chapter II (pp. 29 f.). In the article by Schoenberg referred to above (p. 97) this tendency is elevated to the position of a basic principle, the primary source of the premises of set-structure and set-association. The exclusion of repeated notes and the use of all twelve notes in the construction of the set are explained as motivated by the composer's desire to avoid octave doublings, and there is no reference whatever to the remarkable integrative properties of the combinatorial set, which is proposed merely as a means of facilitating avoidance of the octave when two set-forms are presented simultaneously. Schoenberg's own works offer ample evidence of the speciousness of these explanations of their technical basis. The octave doublings that are freely employed throughout the *Piano Concerto* entail no revision of the postulates of set-structure, and the principle of the combinatorial association of different set-forms is applied as consistently in this composition as in those works of Schoenberg in which the octave simultaneity does not occur.[8]

It is clear that Schoenberg is mistaken in advancing as an explanation of his principles of set-structure and combinatoriality the considerations that motivate his avoidance of the octave: "To double is to emphasize, and an emphasized tone could be interpreted as a root, or even as a tonic; the consequences of such an interpretation must be avoided. Even a slight reminiscence of the former tonal harmony would be disturbing, because it would create false expectations of consequences and continuations."[9] Octave doublings need not necessarily create tonal implications, however; but even where they do not, they may still be objectionable. The simultaneous statement of identical notes derived from two different set-forms may have an

EXAMPLE 146

Schoenberg, Violin Concerto, Op. 36

Copyright 1939 by G. Schirmer, Inc., New York.
Used by permission.

---

[8]In a brief note appended to this article in 1946 Schoenberg refers to the fact that in some of his later works the "rule" against octave doublings is not observed. He does not realize, apparently, that the abrogation of this "rule" invalidates many of the main arguments presented in the article itself.

[9]Schoenberg, *Style and Idea,* p. 219.

effect analogous to that of the cross relation in tonal music, possibly because the linear structure of the respective sets is thereby obscured. It is possible that, in general, avoidance of the octave — the one interval that invariably entails an evaluation of harmonic quality — is motivated by the composer's rejection, in certain contexts, of harmonic criteria based on such an evaluation (see pp. 30 f.).

A certain inconsistency in some compositions in which Schoenberg carefully excludes the octave as a simultaneity would seem to result from his employment in these same works of octave repetitions of set-segments or of individual notes or chords. The harmonic effect of these oblique relations of the octave would presumably be analogous to that produced by octave doublings. (See exx. 96, *b*, 96, *c*, and 146.)

VIII. THE TABULATION OF NONEQUIVALENT PITCH-CLASS COLLECTIONS

The absence of a priori restrictions governing simultaneity in atonal music led Hába and other early commentators on this music to consider its harmonic resources in terms of the number of nonequivalent "chords" available. (Equivalent chords are understood here as collections of identical relative pitch-class content. Thus, all transpositions and all vertical permutations of a given chord are defined as representations of the same chord.) In my article "The Possible Chords in Twelve-Tone Music" I attempted to correct errors in their tabulations of these chords. The discussion that follows[10] is taken from this article. ("Inversion" in the quoted excerpt stands for "harmonic inversion," that is, vertical permutation.)

Since only the content of each chord is to be specified and not the particular order of arrangement of the notes constituting the chord, the elements which remain after each of the different three-note chords is in turn subtracted from the chromatic scale will constitute all the different nine-note chords, and vice-versa. Similarly, the number of eight-note combinations will be identical with the number of four-note combinations, the number of seven-note combinations with the number of five-note combinations, etc., the only unique figure being the number of six-note chords.

The proper symmetry is displayed in the following table of the number of chords in general, that is, including all transpositions:

---

[10]Reprinted from *The Score*, September, 1954, pp. 54 ff., with the kind permission of the editor.

[1 zero-note "chord"][11]   [1 twelve-note chord]
12 one-note "chords"   12 eleven-note chords
66 two-note chords   66 ten-note chords
220 three-note chords   220 nine-note chords
495 four-note chords   495 eight-note chords
792 five-note chords   792 seven-note chords
                  924 six-note chords

The theorem which determines the above figures is as follows: "*The number of combinations of n different things taken r at a time equals the number of permutations of n different things taken r at a time, divided by r!*"[12] In the present instance n is 12, of course, and r is the number of notes in the chord. The symbol $r!$ represents the product of r multiplied by all the positive integers lower than r. If we wish to determine the number of four-note chords, for example, we must first find the number of permutations of twelve different notes taken four at a time and divide this result by 4 x 3 x 2 x 1, or 24. The formula for finding the number of permutations is $n\,(n-1)\,(n-2)\ldots(n-r+1)$. In connection with our four-note chords this means 12 x 11 x 10 x 9, or 11,880. Dividing by 24 we get 495, the total number of four-note chords, including transpositions. But if we wish to find the number of *different* chords we must exclude transpositions, which would apparently be the result of a further division by 12. But 495 divided by 12 is 41¼, which obviously cannot be correct since the number of four-note combinations would necessarily be a whole number. The mystery is solved when we realize that there are three chords which divide the octave symmetrically in such a way that the sum of their transpositions (we include the identity operation) is 1¼ of 12:

c-c♯-f♯-g (6 transpositions)
c-d-f♯-g♯ (6 transpositions)
c-e♭-f♯-a (3 transpositions)

We arrive at our final result, 43, therefore, by subtracting 1¼ from the above quotient and adding 3 to the difference. And this determines that the number of possible eight-note chords, excluding transpositions, must also be 43.

---

[11]For the sake of mathematical completeness, the zero-note "chord" and the twelve-note chord are added to the original tables, as suggested by Roberto Gerhard in his "Reply to George Perle," *The Score*, September, 1954, pp. 59 f. Mr. Gerhard's remarks concerning Hauer's tropes were based on a misunderstanding. He failed to realize that the inversion of a given set is not, in Hauer's system, necessarily a representation of the same trope as the prime form of the set. The two tropes illustrated in example 147, for instance, are inversions of each other's segmental content but are nevertheless classified as independent tropes by Hauer, since the segmental pitch content of the one set is not identical with that of the other set, regardless of the respective pitch levels of the two sets. See pp. 5 f.

[12]William L. Hart, *College Algebra* (New York: D. C. Heath and Company, 1938), Chap. XX.

We reach precisely the same solution if we adopt another, purely "musical" method, involving no algebraic formulæ and no mathematical calculations except addition. To the following base of three notes

$$c\text{-}c\sharp\text{-}d$$

we add in turn each of the remaining notes of the chromatic scale except b, which is omitted since it provides no new chord but merely a transposed inversion (c-$c\sharp$-d-b) of the first chord (c-$c\sharp$-d-$e\flat$). There are thus eight different combinations which will be based upon the same three-note group. Let us maintain the c-$c\sharp$ as a sub-base and generate a third element by raising the pitch of the latter a semitone for each series of operations. The following additional dissimilar combinations will result:

BASE	4TH NOTE	NO. OF COMBINATIONS
c-$c\sharp$-$d\sharp$	e to $b\flat$	7
c-$c\sharp$-e	f to $b\flat$	6
c-$c\sharp$-f	$f\sharp$ to $b\flat$	5
c-$c\sharp$-$f\sharp$	g to $b\flat$	4
c-$c\sharp$-g	a to $b\flat$	2
c-$c\sharp$-$g\sharp$	$b\flat$	1

There are no more combinations including a semitone and we must be on guard to exclude this interval and its inversion in subsequent operations. The combinations c-$c\sharp$-g-$g\sharp$ and c-$c\sharp$-$g\sharp$-a are excluded because they are transposed inversions of earlier constructions (c-$c\sharp$-f-$f\sharp$ and c-$c\sharp$-e-f, respectively). The next step is to raise the second element and to operate as above upon a new sub-base:

BASE	4TH NOTE	NO. OF COMBINATIONS
c-d-e	$f\sharp$ to a	4
c-d-f	g to a	3
c-d-$f\sharp$	$g\sharp$ to a	2

At this point the combinations which contain a whole-step are exhausted and again it becomes necessary to raise the second element:

BASE	4TH NOTE	NO. OF COMBINATIONS
c-$e\flat$-$g\flat$	a	1

It will be seen that further operations can generate only transposed inversions of chords already given, and that the number of four-note chords discovered is 43, as confirmed by the algebraic procedure. Whichever method we adopt will prove the following table of differently constituted chords to be correct:[13]

---

[13]I originally contrived this table by working out all the chords and totalling the results, as explained above, and was surprised to learn that Mr. Pohlmann Mallalieu, at that time a student at the University of Louisville, had independently arrived at the same figures by means of the algebraic method, which he was kind enough to explain. The nonequivalent pitch-class collections, classified in terms of certain general properties, are given in the Appendix.

[1 zero-note "chord"]   [1 twelve-note chord]
1 one-note "chord"   1 eleven-note chord
6 two-note chords   6 ten-note chords
19 three-note chords   19 nine-note chords
43 four-note chords   43 eight-note chords
66 five-note chords   66 seven-note chords
80 six-note chords

The foregoing table of the number of possible chords is also a table of the number of unordered set-segments, since a set-segment is merely a precompositional linear arrangement of the content of a possible chord. The eighty six-note segments were originally tabulated by Hauer and are the basis of his twelve-tone system. Each of Hauer's tropes consists of two hexachords of mutually exclusive content, so that each pair of hexachords includes all twelve notes of the semitonal scale. Only eight hexachords may be associated in this way with their own transpositions. These generate the six tropes illustrated in example 160 and the inversionally complementary pair given in example 147. Each of the remaining seventy-two hexachords must be paired with a dissimilar hexachord in order to form a trope. Thirty-six additional tropes are thus generated, so that the total number of tropes is forty-four. Every one of the 479,001,600 possible permutations of the twelve notes is equivalent, in terms of its hexachordal pitch-class content, to one of these tropes.[14]

EXAMPLE 147

The difficulties of applying the "rule" (discussed on pp. 2 and 72) that only one series should be used in a twelve-tone composition are removed, so far as Schoenberg's work is concerned, if this term is replaced by "trope." Where Berg uses several sets in a composition, however, these are not usually derivable from a single trope. (The first movement of the *Lyric Suite* is an exception; see p. 72.) The rule that a single trope should be used throughout a composition does not apply to Hauer's own music.

---

[14]A table of the 44 tropes is given in Hauer, *Vom Melos zur Pauke* (Vienna, 1925), p. 12.

Since in atonal music collections that are mutually complementary by inversion are generally understood to be different aspects of a single formation, a further reduction in the list of possible chords is in order. The following table omits, therefore, not only the previously excluded categories (transpositions and vertical permutations), but also one member of each pair of mutually invertible chords.

1	zero-note "chord"	1	twelve-note chord
1	one-note "chord"	1	eleven-note chord
6	two-note chords	6	ten-note chords
12	three-note chords	12	nine-note chords
29	four-note chords	29	eight-note chords
38	five-note chords	38	seven-note chords

50 six-note chords

VI

Structural Functions
of the Set

Schoenberg and many of his followers have often depended upon the traditional forms to provide models for the overall organization of their twelve-tone works. In some of Schoenberg's works this dependence affects the smaller formal elements as well, to the extent that "antecedent" and "consequent" phrases of four bars each appear, consistently paired to form "periods," combined with similar constructions to form "phrase-groups," and so forth (see ex. 82).[1]

Set-structure under these circumstances plays only a secondary role or none at all in the formal organization of the work, the formal function of the set being essentially limited to that of providing, in addition to a certain homogeneity of texture, thematic elements whose individuality depends upon the various ways in which restatements of the set may be compositionally differentiated from one another. The contrasting procedures used in the disposition of the notes of the set are the source of the first and second subjects of Schoenberg's *Klavierstück*, Opus 33a (ex. 148). The larger formal components are characterized by the exposition, recurrence, and modification of these "thematic" statements of the set.

---

[1]Schoenberg himself insists that the traditional formal relationships are dependent upon the functional harmonies of the major-minor system in *Structural Functions of Harmony* (New York: W. W. Norton and Company, 1954), particularly in the lengthy chapter "Progressions for Various Compositional Purposes." In their attempts to prove that the new music is historically a continuation of the old, however, Schoenberg and other writers ignore the harmonic basis of the conventional forms and grossly exaggerate the formal function of traditional motivic operations. The clearly fundamental role performed by the set as the source of pitch relations in twelve-tone music is equated with a supposedly parallel function attributed to the motive in tonal music.

EXAMPLE 148

The formal subdivisions of Opus 33*a* are clarified through the subjection of the set to different types of segmentation, as indicated in the following suggested outline of the overall formal scheme (the figures in the column at the right represent the number of notes in each segment).

EXPOSITION

I.	First Group	
	A. Subject I (bars 1-2)	4/4/4
	B. Episode (bars 3-9)	4/4/4
	C. Modified return of Subject I (bars 10-11)	4/4/4
	D. Transition (bars 12-13)	4/4/4
II.	Second Group	
	A. Subject II (bars 14-18)	6/6
	B. Episode (bars 19-20)	6/4
	C. Modified return of Subject II (bar 21 to beginning of bar 23)[2]	/6
	D. Codetta and transition (second half of bar 23 through fifth eighth-note value of bar 27)	3/3/3/3

DEVELOPMENT

I.	(Conclusion of bar 27 to middle of bar 29)	Various types of segments
II.	(Conclusion of bar 29 to *fermata*, bar 32)	4/4/4

RECAPITULATION

I.	Modified return of Subject I (following *fermata*, bar 32, through bar 34)	4/4/4
II.	(Modified return of Subject II (bars 35-36)	6/6

CODA

I.	(bars 37-38)	4/4/4
II.	(bar 39, including upbeat through bar 40)	4/4/4

The harmonic formation commencing in the second half of bar 23 (ex. 149) calls attention to the important role assigned to the interval of the perfect fifth throughout the work: the set is semi-combinatorial, with the combinatorial relation based on the pairing of P-0 and I-5, so that the initial note of I is a perfect fifth below that of P; the first and final notes of the set are separated by

---

[2] For B and C of this group see example 149, where the incomplete statements of the set that occur in these two sections are illustrated. Note the discrepancy in bar 22, an *a*♮ in the right-hand part instead of *ab*, as "required" by the second segment of P-0. Another discrepancy will be noted in the left-hand part of the same bar, the omission of the *a*♮ "required" by I-5. The conclusion that this "missing" note has been transferred to the right-hand part is completely inconsistent not only with Schoenberg's practice in the remainder of this piece but with his practice in general. If the *a*♮ is taken to be a misprint for *ab*, one irregularity (a missing *a*♮) replaces two (a missing *ab* and an interpolation). It is possible that the *ab* is omitted here in order to enhance the cadential effect of the sustained fifth, *ab-eb*, in the following bar (cf. the discussion below of bars 19-24). An indubitable error is found at the conclusion of bar 35: the repeated note in the left-hand part should read *bb*.

EXAMPLE 149

a tritone, the only interval that will permit the initial vertical relationship between P and I to occur also between the final note of P and the final note of I; the set commences with two conjunct fifths, so that this three-note unit is found at the beginning of P and I and at the conclusion of R and RI; the omission from the set-statements in bar 19 to the beginning of bar 23 of the fifths enclosed in parentheses in example 149 gives this interval additional weight upon its eventual appearance in bars 23-24. Since the commencement and conclusion of almost every phrase coincide with the commencement and conclusion of one or of a pair of set-forms, the position of the perfect fifth in the set clearly establishes it as the dominating intervallic relationship. As such, it determines the transpositional levels of the set-statements. In the exposition the two combinatorial pairs, P-0 and I-5, R-0 and RI-5, remain untransposed; in the development the whole group is first transposed to the second fifth above, then to the first fifth above; the recapitulation commences with another descent of a fifth, restoring the original "key," which is maintained to the end. The transpositional scheme is thus an expansion of the initial three-note unit of the set.

Among the factors that complicate the transference of traditional formal schemes to twelve-tone composition is the quasi-motivic character of the Schoenbergian set (see p. 5). The thematic operations that characterize the traditional formal structures in the major-minor system occur within a functional context that they do not determine. Among the distinctive features of the tonal theme the most important is its ordering of melodic intervals, an ordering that retains its individual character in spite of changes in mode, harmony, and tonality. The ordering of pitch relations in the set, however, establishes the frame of reference within which the theme must move. The *theme* of a twelve-tone work, therefore, is not in general characterized by its intervallic structure but by attributes that formerly performed a subsidiary, though essential, role: rhythm, texture, dynamics, color, shape (the last defined only in the most general terms, as in the following discussion of the thematic implications of the contour of the initial motive of Opus 33*a*). In a sense, every twelve-tone work is in variation form, and the formal problem in each consists of the comprehensive organization of a series of variations through the superimposition of a special structural scheme, whether that scheme is externally analogous to the traditional forms or is a novel arrangement.

The foregoing outline of the formal plan of Opus 33*a* must be regarded merely as an approximate description of certain superficial structural features. The integrative rhythmic procedures, for example, must also be indicated. The following are a few salient rhythmic details: the progressive elaboration, through the subdivision of the beat into smaller values, of the three statements of Subject I; the gradually increasing momentum of the measures that intervene between the original presentation of Subject I and the *poco rit.* that leads to its first restatement, achieved initially through a progressive increase in the number of attacks in each phrase-segment and then through the change to notes of lesser duration (bars 3–8); the interrupted sixteenth-note pattern of the transitional passages (bars 8–9, 12–13, 26, the development section); the regular eighth-note pattern of Subject II. The melodic contour and harmonic content of the first two bars are even more significant unifying elements. The essential shape of the whole movement is microcosmically contained in the melodic arch of the first two bars, the contour of which is imitated in the broader time span of bars 3–7, restored to its original duration but spatially expanded in bars 10–11, both temporally and spatially expanded at the beginning of the recapitulation. The six chords of the initial figure, derived from the direct succession of P–0 and RI–5 (ex. 148, *a*), are a statement of the primary harmonic material of the composition. (The direct succession of these two set-forms presents a "secondary set," as explained in the preceding chapter, p. 100.)

The compositional importance of the interval of a fifth in Opus 33*a* is a consequence of the structure of the set, not of any quality inherent in the interval itself. The attribution to this interval of some special a priori significance, implied in Schoenberg's emphasis on relationships based on the fifth in almost all of his twelve-tone works, can only be explained as an unjustified transference of tonal concepts. His consistent use of this interval between the initial notes of combinatorially paired P and I set-forms has already been mentioned. But the initial notes of combinatorially paired set-forms may just as easily present any other interval containing an odd number of semitones. The properties of the set are in no way dependent upon the interval required to establish a combinatorial relation between P and I. Rufer explains Schoenberg's preference for the fifth as the initial interval of the combinatorial aggregate as indicating "the presence of a principle, or at any rate a method of procedure, which uses the natural acoustical relations of notes for the additional strengthening of the musical material."[3] But in general no special emphasis is given to the initial interval between P and I in the compositional presentation of the material, so that this "natural acoustical relation" is not *heard* as such. One need only state the combinatorial pair in reverse, as R and RI, to get a new initial interval (except in the special instance of a set so constructed that its first and last notes are separated by the tritone). According to Schoenberg's own "law of the unity of musical space,"[4] either presentation is in itself as valid as the other.

The structural function of transpositions at the fifth in diatonic music does not depend upon the "natural" character of this interval but upon the fact that in the diatonic system a hierarchy of relationships is generated by such

---

[3]Rufer, *Composition with Twelve Notes* (New York, 1954), p. 134.
[4]Schoenberg, *Style and Idea*, p. 223.

transpositions. Analogous possibilities are offered by certain types of set-structure, the different pitch levels that would be required for the realization of these possibilities being in each instance dependent upon this structure and upon no other considerations. The set of Schoenberg's *Third Quartet* is especially interesting from this point of view. The six discrete dyads into which the set may be segmented are merely interchanged, the content of each dyad remaining invariant, under the following operations: P-0, P-6, I-3, I-9 (and the corresponding retrograde forms). These four forms of the set can conceivably be employed to establish a specific region of tone relations—a "home key," so to speak (ex. 150, *a*). Modulatory possibilities are presented by the appearance of a new series of six interchangeable dyads through the association of a cyclic permutation of P-0 with the equivalent permutation of I-7 (ex. 150, *b*).

EXAMPLE 150

The formal possibilities of this set, however, are not exploited by Schoenberg. Although the concept of combinatoriality does not appear, the principal set-forms employed are, as in the later works, the prime and its inversion at the perfect fifth below. But in this instance these two set-forms bear no special relationship to one another, either through similarity or differentiation of segmental content. The choice of this interval is not motivated by considerations of set-structure. A similar dependence on traditional concepts is evidenced in the formal plan of the work, in the relation between "accompaniment" and "melody," and so on.

The axiomatic transformation procedures of the twelve-tone system are sometimes employed as the basis of overall structure (see p. 104), of thematic operations (see p. 62), or of contrasting formal elements. The "unity of musical space" (see p. 116) implied in the precompositional operations automatically permits the total inversion of a formal component, as in the first movement of the *Third Quartet*, a quasi-sonata whose recapitulation presents the inversion of "theme II" followed by that of "theme I," at a transpositional level that permits the retention of the principal sets of the exposition, P-0 and I-5. Different movements of a work may be derived from different set-forms, as in Krenek's *Suite for Violoncello Solo*, the first four movements of which are each based on a different aspect of the set, and the fifth and final movement on the combined use of all four aspects. The precompositional relationships directly determine the overall musical structure in the third movement of Berg's *Lyric Suite* and in the "Sextet" from Act I and "Film Music" from Act II of *Lulu*. The first of these is a special variant of *da capo* form, with the return of the first section taking place in the retrograde. In the "Sextet" and "Film Music" a literal retrograde restatement commences at the exact midpoint of the movement.

Recurrent successions of set-forms constitute the formal basis of the first movement of Webern's *String Trio*, Opus 20. The succession of sets is arranged in five different series, as follows:

> A: P-0, R-0
> B: RI-6, I-11, P-0, I-1, RI-4, I-10, (P-11)
> C: P-3, RI-10, R-8, R-3
> D: RI-0, R-1, I-8, RI-4, R-2, R-4, P-4
> E: R-0

The overall structure of the movement, in terms of the succession of set-statements, is as follows: A B C B D D A B C B E. This scheme represents only the material substructure of the work, not the procedures employed in the compositional disposition of this material. The principle of perpetual variation operates throughout, sectional repetitions being characterized only through a few salient motivic and rhythmic elements, such as those at the beginning of each B section (ex. 151). It is not evident that any particular principle governs the choice of set-forms, in spite of the fact that the structure of the set suggests possible criteria of selection.

The formal implications of set-structure are more clearly realized in several later works by Webern, especially the *Symphony*, Opus 21, in two movements. The set, example 152, consists of two six-note subsets, the second of which is a literal retrograde of the first at the tritone. Each transposition of the prime and of the inverted set is therefore identical with the tritone transposition of its respective retrograde form, so that the set-complex comprises only twenty-four rather than forty-eight nonequivalent members.

Each of the three sections of the first movement (bars 1-26, 25-44, 43-66) is a double canon by inversion. The appearance of strict canonic forms in a twelve-tone work is in itself no indication of any remarkable ingenuity on the part of the composer, since the relationships that define these forms are automatically provided by the precompositional operations of the twelve-tone system. The exploitation of these relationships is meaningful, therefore, only to the extent that rhythmic, motivic, textural, and harmonic elements function as additional criteria of association and contrast.

The first double canon (ex. 155, bars 1-26) is derived through the pairing of an inverted set with each statement of a prime set, all the inversional relationships being based on a single axis of symmetry, the note *a*, with which the work commences. With the exception of *eb*, the tritone of this note, each note retains its original octave position, regardless of the set-form of which it is a component (ex. 153). Two octave positions will necessarily be available for the tritone of the axis of symmetry.

EXAMPLE 151

EXAMPLE 152

EXAMPLE 153

The linear succession of set-forms is determined by intersection, the last two notes of P overlapping the first two of the appropriately transposed I set, and vice versa. The structure of the set generates invariant dyadic relations between these linearly combined set-forms (ex. 154). The invariant dyads thus formed, together with other invariant formations among the vertically com-

EXAMPLE 154

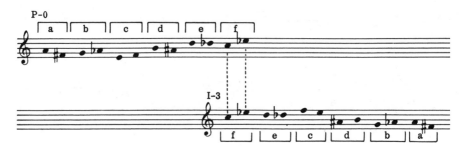

bined set-forms, permit the appearance of recurrent melodic cells. These cells are additionally characterized by the constant octave position of each note and by rhythmic means. Compare, for instance, in example 155, the melodic interval *g-ab* in bars 3-4 with the same interval in bars 9-10, the *b-bb* in bars 5-6 and bars 7-8, the *d-c♯* in bar 10 and bar 13.

A primary integrative function is assigned to rhythm in this work. An overall rhythmic scheme governs the distribution of attacks and of durational values in each section. The rhythmic structure of the first canon is indicated in example 156. (The durational symbols in ex. 156 indicate where, in a measure, a new note is attacked in any part.)

In the second double canon, beginning at bar 25, the rhythmic pattern of each of the two antecedent voices is identical, so that, simultaneously with the double canon by inversion of the melodic intervals, there unfolds a single four-part rhythmic canon. The second half of the second double canon (bars 35-44) is a literal retrograde of its first half (ex. 155, bars 25-34).

Registral contrast is employed as one of the means of formal articulation. Both canons of the first section are restricted to the same fixed octave positions within the middle and low registers (ex. 153), and both canons of the third section to the same fixed octave positions within the middle and high registers. The second section, in contrast, has one of its canons assigned to the middle and high and the other to the middle and low registers, with the overall compass approximating that of the two outer sections together.

"Harmonic" structure is represented by the assignment of the same inversionally complementary pairs of pitch classes to all paired P and I sets within each section, the final double canon functioning, in this sense, as a recapitulation of the first (in both outer sections the sum of each pair of complementary pitches is 0, or 12),[5] and the middle double canon serving as a contrasting section by virtue of its restatement of these complementary pairs at T-7 (so that the sum of each pair of complementary pitches is 14, or 2). For further illustrations of the pairing of inversionally related set-forms in terms of a common sum of complementation the reader is referred to the second movement of Webern's *Variations* for piano, Opus 27[6], and the *Quartet*, Opus 22 (see pp. 134 f., below).

The second movement of the *Symphony* (Op. 21), comprising "Thema," seven variations, and "Coda," derives the formal plan of each section and of the movement as a whole from the symmetrical structure of the set. The relationship of prime to retrograde of the two constituent subsets (ex. 152) strictly determines the form of each section, with the exception of Variation IV; that variation is the axis of an overall quasi-symmetrical structure based on correspondences between "Thema" and "Coda" (ex. 157), variations I and VII, II and VI, and III and V.

The symmetrical relationships are presented in a unique manner in this central variation (ex. 158): rhythmic elements and elements of timbre are restated in reverse order from the midpoint of the section, as in each of the

---

[5]See p. 3, above.

[6]See Peter Westergaard, "Webern and 'Total Organization': An Analysis of the Second Movement of Piano Variations, Op. 27," *Perspectives of New Music,* I/2 (1963), 107 ff.; and Roy Travis, "Directed Motion in Schoenberg and Webern," *ibid.*, IV/2 (1966), pp. 87 ff. Example 153, above, is derived from Mr. Travis' article and replaces example 134 of the first edition of this book. The new version illustrates the role that Webern assigns to the circle of fifths in establishing the fixed octave positions of bars 1-26 of the first movement of the *Symphony.*

EXAMPLE 155

[cont d on p. 123]

EXAMPLE 155 [cont'd]

EXAMPLE 156

other variations, but the internal order of some melodic figures is directly restated, with only the overall succession of these figures reversed, while the internal order of the remaining melodic figures is reversed, with the overall succession of these figures directly restated. The invariant dyadic relations shown in example 154 are thus compositionally projected. The strict linear unfolding of each set-statement in example 158 is interrupted only in bar 50, which is the exact midpoint of the movement, with 49 bars on either side. The final segments of I-4, I-2, P-3, and P-1 overlap at this point with, respectively, the initial segments of P-1, P-11, I-6, and I-4.

It has been pointed out that *every* twelve-tone work consists of variations on a twelve-tone set. The use of the term "variation form" to designate the formal structure of an individual twelve-tone work, therefore, presumably implies the presence of a special referential idea. In the present instance the referential character of the "Thema" resides in its length—eleven bars—and in its symmetrical structure, two features which recur in each of the succeeding variations. Another type of variation procedure is found in the first movement of Webern's *II. Kantate*, Opus 31. The total melodic and harmonic content of the movement is presented in bars 1-12; each succeeding section (bars 12-25

EXAMPLE 157

EXAMPLE 158

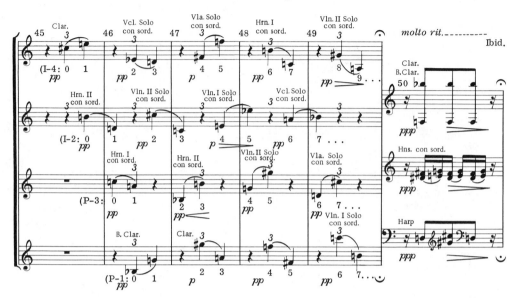

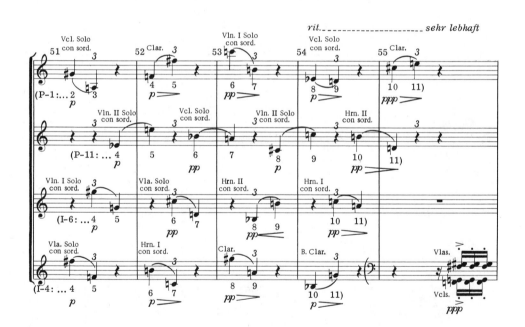

and 25–44) modifies only the rhythm, dynamics, and spacing of the melodic and harmonic elements initially derived from the set; a four-measure coda presents a final variation of the salient chord and melodic motive (ex. 130) with which each of the preceding sections commences.

Various methods that have been described in preceding chapters for the derivation of motivic and harmonic elements from the set are capable of expansion and elaboration at several levels and may ultimately function as the basis of the formal scheme. To the extent that a particular device is capable of integrating the melodic and harmonic content of a work it is also capable of organizing the overall structural relations. The form-producing possibilities inherent in the set, therefore, have already been implied in earlier discussions of its linear and harmonic functions.

The formal possibilities of a special type of set-structure are already realized to a certain extent in the twelve-tone sections of the "Tanzscene" from Schoenberg's Opus 24 (see pp. 94 f.). These sections are based entirely on a closed system of relations between set-forms, generated by an unordered semi-combinatorial set in which the hexachordal content remains constant at the tritone transposition (exx. 134 and 135). The expanded combinatorial relations generated by an all-combinatorial set enlarge the reciprocal relations among the forms of the set and, therefore, the means of formal development within an integrated structure as well. From a set of the type illustrated in example 141, for instance, one may derive eight set-forms that are equivalent in terms of hexachordal content. Each set-form may be combinatorially paired with one transposition of each transformation of the set, where the aggregate structure is based on the association of corresponding hexachords, and with another transposition where the aggregate structure is based on the association of noncorresponding hexachords. A total of sixteen nonequivalent pairs of set-forms is thus generated in the former case, and of twenty nonequivalent pairs in the latter. Linear progression by means of secondary sets may be developed through successive statements of set-forms in thirty-two different ways. The principle of combinatoriality permits a similarly comprehensive description of the precompositional resources generated by any specific set.

Schoenberg's premise of a precompositional ordering of the notes makes it possible to define a nonsegmented set consisting of all the notes of the semitonal scale (see p. 5). The combinatorial set is characterized further by the specific content of its segments, and thus provides the possibility of a revision of the premised order (as in the *String Trio*) and even of a rejection of the premise itself (as in the *Ode to Napoleon*), in the interest of linear variety. In Schoenberg's later work, invariant segmental content rather than linear ordering must be regarded as the essential property that defines the set.[7] We-

---

[7] There are two isolated early instances of Schoenberg's use of unordered segmented sets, but in both the set is used episodically, as a momentary device within a nonserial context. The first of these is referred to in a letter from Schoenberg to Nicolas Slonimsky, printed in *Music Since 1900* (New York: Charles Scribner's Sons, 1971), pp. 1315 f.: "The first step happened about

bern, however, insists on a strict adherence to the preestablished order. Webern's inviolable precompositional ordering and Schoenberg's inviolable segmental content are both retained as initial premises of Babbitt's combinatorial
procedures. Without the premise of ordered succession there is no means of
distinguishing among the members of the complex of set-forms generated, as
in example 141, by the all-combinatorial set, the properties of which, at the
same time, derive from the premise of invariant segmental content.

The disposition of these set-forms in the first movement of Babbitt's *Three
Compositions for Piano*, which is based on example 141, is indicated in the
following table. The vertical alignment of set-forms in the table indicates that
they are combinatorially associated through the simultaneous statement of
corresponding hexachords; the diagonal alignment indicates that they are
associated through the simultaneous statement of noncorresponding segments.
Examples 142 and 159 may be compared with the relevant parts of the table.
Secondary sets determine the horizontal succession of set-forms throughout,
except at certain "dead" intervals (indicated by a slant line in the table)
separating the larger formal components. In terms of the arrangement of
set-forms, the overall structure is a canon in retrograde, sections four and five
stating in reverse succession the reversed set-forms of sections three and two,
respectively, at their original transpositional level, and section six stating in
reverse succession the reversed set-forms of section one at the tritone transposition.

SECTION ONE (bars 1-8):

P-6	R-0	RI-7	I-1
P-0	RI-1	I-7	R-6

SECTION TWO (bars 9-18):

	R-0	I-1	I-1	R-0	RI-7		P-6	P-6	RI-7
P-0	RI-1	RI-1		I-7	P-0	R-6	I-7	R-6/

SECTION THREE (bars 19-28):

I-1	R-0		R-0				
P-6 RI-7 P-6			I-1		P-6	P-6 RI-7/	
		R-0	RI-7	RI-7	I-1	R-0	I-1/

SECTION FOUR (bars 29-38):

RI-1 P-0 RI-1		I-7 I-7		P-0		
I-7 R-6		R-6		RI-1	R-6 I-7	R-6/
				P-0	P-0 RI-1	

December 1914 or at the beginning of 1915 when I sketched a symphony, the last part of which
became later the 'Jakobsleiter,' but which has never been continued. The Scherzo of this
symphony was based on a theme consisting of the twelve tones. But this was only one of the
themes. I was still far away from the idea to use such a basic theme as a unifying means for a
whole work." The relevant passage is reproduced in Leibowitz, *Introduction à la musique de
douze sons* (Paris: L'arche, 1949), pp. 50 f., and Humphrey Searle, *Twentieth Century Counterpoint* (London: Williams and Norgate, 1954), pp. 77 f. See also Winfried Zillig, "Notes on

SECTION FIVE (bars 39-48):

	P-6	RI-7	P-6	R-0	RI-7		I-1	I-1	R-0/
I-7	R-6	R-6		I-7	P-0	RI-1	RI-1	P-0/	

SECTION SIX (bars 49-56):

P-0	RI-1	I-7	R-6
RI-7	I-1	P-6	R-0

The canonic arrangement of the material is not literally reflected in the compositional superstructure (cf. ex. 142, *b*, comprising the last five set-statements of section three, with ex. 159, comprising the first five set-statements of section four).

EXAMPLE 159

Babbitt (1947)

The combinatorial properties of a set are dependent not on the order of the notes within the segment but only on the content of the segment. Any set whose segmental content is identical with that of P-0 of example 141 or a transposition thereof will present exactly analogous relationships among the members of the set-complex which it generates. Every combinatorial set may be similarly characterized precompositionally in terms of its segmental content. All semi-combinatorial sets of the Schoenbergian type (see pp. 96 f.) are, in terms of their segmental content, reducible to only thirteen different "tropes"[8] or, as Babbitt prefers to designate them, "source sets." The all-combinatorial sets are merely ordered arrangements of an even smaller number of source sets, characterized by the properties described in the preceding chapter (p. 98). These sets are illustrated in example 160 (the specific permutation and pitch level are arbitrary).

The analogous source sets based on four-note and three-note segments (see p. 98) are illustrated in example 161. Each of these, like the bisected all-combinatorial sets (ex. 160), is statable at several transpositional levels without revision of segmental content.

Arnold Schoenberg's Unfinished Oratorio, 'Die Jakobsleiter,' " *The Score,* June, 1959, 7 ff. The second instance was cited above on pp. 94 f.

[8]See Appendix.

EXAMPLE 160

(1)

(2)

(3)

(4)

(5)

(6)

EXAMPLE 161

a.

(1)

(2)

(3)

(4)

(5)

(6)

[cont d on p. 131]

EXAMPLE 161 [cont'd]

b.

Special types of set-structure will permit the derivation, from a single set, of several classes of combinatorial relations. Both invariant four-note and six-note segments are provided by the following set,[9] which is simultaneously representative of source set (3) of example 160 and source set (2) of example 161, *a*. Through corresponding six-note segments, P-0 may be combinatorially associated with P-3, I-9, R-0, or RI-6; through corresponding four-note segments P-0 may be combinatorially associated with P-2 and P-4, RI-7 and RI-5, P-2 and RI-7, P-4 and RI-5. Any one of the above set-forms may be replaced by its tritone transposition without affecting the combinatorial relationships.

EXAMPLE 162

P-0

Babbitt stresses the importance of the

hierarchy of relationships [that] exists among the source sets as determinants of regions, an hierarchical domain closely analogous to the "circle of fifths," and defined similarly by considering the minimum number and the nature of the pitch alterations necessary to reproduce source sets at various transpositional levels. For example, in set (4) [ex. 160], the transposition of note C by a tritone—the excluded interval—or the similar transposition of the symmetrically related note F, reproduces the set structure a half step lower in the latter case, or a half step higher in the former case, with

---

[9]From *Three Inventions for Piano*, No. 3, by George Perle.

maximum association of content to the original set. Thus, any degree of motion away from the pitch norm is measurable. Also, the motion from the region whose structure is defined by one such source set to that defined by another source set is achieved and measured in precisely the same manner. For example, the transposition of the note C♯ in set (4) by a tritone results in set (5); likewise, the symmetrically related E, when so transposed, results in set (5). These properties suggest that whether the source sets are used as specific compositional sets or not, they possess properties of so general a nature as to warrant their presence as implicit structural entities.[10]

Derived sets offer a means of progression within this "hierarchy of relationships." It will be noted that, in terms of hexachordal content, the fundamental set and the derived sets illustrated in examples 116 and 117 are representations of source set (4), transposed, of example 160. The interchange of the second and third subsets transforms example 117, *a* and *b*, into representations of source set (2), transposed. In terms of its hexachordal content the set of Webern's *Concerto for Nine Instruments* (ex. 111) is a representation of source set (2). The interchange of the second and fourth subsets would transform this set into a representation of source set (4).[11]

Babbitt has shown that the primary operations of the twelve-tone system may be applied not only in the organization of pitch relations but also in the organization of rhythmic relations.[12] This concept is already foreshadowed in Webern's structural use of rhythmic and other nonpitch elements (see pp. 18, 21 ff., 32, 80, 81, 120 f.) Rhythmic retrogression is, of course, not a novel device, since it occurs in tonal music concomitantly with thematic and formal retrogression, although exclusively in a dependent role, as a component of the thematic pattern. Rhythmic inversion offers a certain conceptual difficulty if this term is understood to signify a directional operation, the turning "upside down" of a series of rhythmic elements. In terms of the permutation of the elements of the set, however, rhythmic inversion of a set of durational values is analogous to inversion of a set of pitches.

An illustration of the nature of these transformations as they apply to the rhythmic set of the first movement of Babbitt's *Three Compositions for Piano*[13] follows. The prime aspect of the rhythmic set is represented by the following series of integers:

$$\text{P:} \quad 5 \quad 1 \quad 4 \quad 2$$

By subtracting each number in turn from a constant of such a value that the

[10]"Some Aspects of Twelve-Tone Composition," *The Score and I.M.A. Magazine*, June 1955, p. 58.

[11]*Ibid.*, pp. 59 f.

[12]*Ibid.*, pp. 60 f.

[13]This work, composed in 1947, is apparently the earliest in which nonpitch components are serialized. It precedes by two years Olivier Messiæn's composition *Modes de valeurs et d'intensités*.

resulting series introduces no elements not already given (the constant in this instance is 6) the inversion is constructed as follows:

$$\text{I:} \quad 1 \quad 5 \quad 2 \quad 4$$

The inversion of a set of pitch elements is an analogous operation, the constant from which the elements of the prime set, notated as pitch numbers, are subtracted being determined by the transposition number of the desired inverted set-form.[14]

The retrograde operation applied to P and I of Babbitt's rhythmic set given above will generate the remaining set-forms:

$$\text{R:} \quad 2 \quad 4 \quad 1 \quad 5$$
$$\text{RI:} \quad 4 \quad 2 \quad 5 \quad 1$$

The unit of reference in the composition is the sixteenth note. Each section of the movement is rhythmically characterized by the means employed to articulate the set of durational values. Each aspect of the set of durational values is uniquely associated with the corresponding aspect of the set of pitch elements. In section one (ex. 142, *a*) the durational values of the set are given by groups of successive sixteenth units, each group being separated from the others by the sustension (variable in length) of its final element or by a rest (also variable). In section two each set of pitch elements is stated twice, once as a series of four three-note chords, each chord being of the durational value required by the rhythmic set (ex. 122), and a second time as twelve successive sixteenth notes, grouped into the required numerical segments by means of slurs. In section three the set is again presented as twelve successive sixteenth notes, rhythmically segmented to conform to the rhythmic set by means of the appropriate distribution of accents (ex. 142, *b*). In section four the four three-note chords return, each stated as a sixteenth unit, with the required durational values completed by means of interpolated rests (ex. 159). In section five each set of pitch elements is alternately stated in the rhythmic guise in which it appeared in each of the two preceding sections. Section six returns to the rhythmic procedure of section one. (An additional rhythmic formation is employed in sections three and four, consisting of twelve successive sixteenth notes without internal rhythmic articulation [exx. 142, *b*, and 159].)[15]

The various ways in which the rhythmic and pitch elements may be correlated with each other offer an additional means of integration and development. In the brief and relatively simple movement examined above there is a one-to-one correlation between the structuralized components: each aspect of

---

[14]See p. 3, above.

[15]Babbitt's more recent notions concerning the serialization of rhythmic elements are described in his article, "Twelve-Tone Rhythmic Structure and the Electronic Medium," *Perspectives of New Music*, I/1 (1962), 49 ff.

the set of pitch-class elements is invariably associated with a specific aspect of the set of durational values. There is an additional one-to-one correlation with a specific dynamic value, as follows: P with *mp*, R with *mf*, I with *f*, RI with *p*. These dynamic values are modified only in the closing section, where the whole group is "transposed" to a new level, two degrees less in intensity, so that P is associated with *pp*, R with *p*, I with *mp*, and RI with *ppp*. More complex types of correlation among the different components are of course entirely feasible and are usually found in Babbitt's work.

A strict adherence to the precompositional assumptions of the twelve-tone system is not necessarily inconsistent with the establishment of tone centers, and may even contribute to this result, as it does in Webern's Opus 22.[16] The first movement employs the following succession of set-statements:

P-0	‖	P-6	P-0	‖	P-9	P-10	R-11	P-11	R-0	P-6	P-0	‖	R-0
I-10	‖	: I-4	I-10 :	‖	: I-1	I-0	RI-11	I-11	RI-10	I-4	I-10 :	‖	RI-10
		(I-0	I-6)							(I-0	I-6)		

With the exception of those shown in parentheses, each set-form is canonically paired with an inversionally related form, the same pairs of complementary pitches being maintained throughout the movement (as indicated by the fact that the sum of transposition numbers for each P and I or R and RI pair is the same, mod 12):

$$
\begin{array}{ccccccc}
f\sharp & f & e & d\sharp & d & c\sharp & c \\
f\sharp & g & g\sharp & a & b\flat & b & c
\end{array}
$$

Through segmentation, choice of octave position, and rhythmic placement of the canonically paired segments, *f♯*, one of the two axes of inversional symmetry, is established as a focal element (cf. ex. 113). *c♯* serves as a co-ordinate focal element in consequence of the articulative procedures that emphasize its position as the initial note of P-0 and I-0 and the final note of P-6, I-6, and R-0. At the climactic midpoint of the movement, both types of centricity converge, *f♯* serving not only as an axis of symmetry but also as an initial or final note of the four set-forms at T-11.

The second movement is a rondo whose formal components are defined by the pitch levels assigned to the set-forms. The principal subject is limited to statements of P-5, RI-5, I-5, and R-5. The transposition number is one that does not occur in the first movement, but the same inversionally complementary pitch relations are preserved, with priority conferred upon the two axes of symmetry, *f♯* and *c*, in consequence of their position as boundaries of the four

---

[16]See Note 12, Chap. IV.

set-forms. The first subordinate subject returns to the T-11 forms that had been employed at the climax of the first movement, so that *f♯* and *c* continue to serve as axes of symmetry and as first or last notes of set-forms. Subsequent sections digress, for the first time, from the complementary pitch relations of the first movement, but the "home key" is repeatedly asserted through the return of set-forms to pitch levels that generate the original pairs of inversionally complementary pitch classes. The concluding section returns to T-5, with the set-forms so disposed as to commence and conclude with the principal tone center, *f♯*:

$$\begin{array}{c} \text{R-5} \\ \text{P-5} \qquad \text{R-5} \\ \text{I-5} \end{array}$$

A comment of Webern's on this movement is reported by a pupil of his: "When we were analyzing the Scherzo of Beethoven's Piano Sonata Op. 14, No. 2, [he said] that during the analysis he had in fact realized that the second movement of his quartet was formally an exact analogy with the Beethoven Scherzo."[17] That Webern conceived of the structural principles on which the rondo is based as in some way analogous to those of traditional tonality is also implied by the internal evidence of the work itself.

It is true that the main developments considered so far in this chapter do not support the belief once expressed by Ernst Krenek, that, "in a later stage of development, atonal music may not need the strict regulations of the twelve-tone technique," and that "the essentials of this technique will grow into a sort of second nature."[18] There are, however, important works — including, among the compositions discussed in the preceding pages, Schoenberg's *Ode to Napoleon* and Berg's *Lulu* — that are not based upon these "strict regulations," but that may still be described as "twelve-tone," a term that conveniently differentiates their technical procedures and general character from those of "free" atonality and at the same time suggests that these works are historically dependent upon both "free" atonality and the "strict" twelve-tone system.

The concept of segmental invariance plays a fundamental role in *Lulu*, in a manner which is consistent with other features of Berg's musical language and with the assumptions that distinguish his twelve-tone method from Schoenberg's (cf. pp. 76-78, above). The basic series *does* have priority among the various sets employed in the opera, but not for the reasons given by Reich, Leibowitz, Searle, and others (cf. p. 74). Among the half-dozen strictly serial sets found in *Lulu*, the most important in terms of their structural significance in the work are given in example 163.

---

[17] Willi Reich, in Webern, *The Path to the New Music* (Bryn Mawr, Pa.: Presser, 1963), p. 57.

[18] Krenek, *Studies in Counterpoint* (New York, 1940), p. ix.

EXAMPLE 163

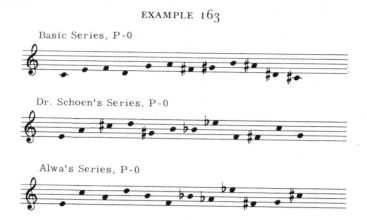

The basic series is unique in that it is the only series in *Lulu* that is all-combinatorial (a representation of source set (6) of example 160). Although Berg does not employ Schoenberg's principle of the setting up of twelve-tone aggregates through the alignment of set-segments that are mutually exclusive in content, the special nature of the all-combinatorial set is nevertheless manifested in the associative possibilities of the basic series.[19]

The primary pair of P and I set-forms of the basic series is shown in example 164. Transpositions at T-6 interchange the content of the two hexachords:

EXAMPLE 164

The most striking evidence of the compositional relevance in *Lulu* of that equivalence of hexachordal content between P and I forms which characterizes the all-combinatorial series is the fact that, with one exception, the basic series is the only strictly serial set in the opera whose P and I forms are associated as structurally equivalent complementary aspects of the series. (The

---

[19]In the context of the present discussion, it is perhaps more appropriate to speak of "all-associative" and "semi-associative," rather than "all-combinatorial" and "semi-combinatorial" sets. (See David Lewin, "A Theory of Segmental Association in Twelve-Tone Music," *Perspectives of New Music*, I/1 [1962], p. 96.)

[20]I sets in *Lulu* that are assigned transposition no. 0 will be understood as having priority over other pitch levels of I. In other words, the transposition no. of I is assigned without reference to the initial element of P-0. Cf. n. 3, Chap. III.

one exception is Lulu's series [ex. 84], which is, however, merely employed as an incidental melodic detail and is thus not a source of segmental pitch-class collections. Even so, it is perhaps worth mentioning that, unlike the other strictly serial sets, Lulu's series is at least semi-combinatorial, the content of one hexachord being inversionally complementary to the other. Since this segmentation is not explicitly emphasized compositionally, it may seem far-fetched to relate this precompositional structural feature to the fact that P and I are employed as structurally equivalent complementary aspects of this series. However, see the comment below on the referential significance that certain pitch-class collections in *Lulu* retain even when they are not explicitly articulated as segments.)

Alwa's series is almost exclusively employed in its prime aspect. The principal referential forms, P-0 and P-5, are each maximally invariant with the principal referential form, P-0, of the basic series, in that corresponding hexachords of the respective set-forms have five notes in common (ex. 165). (The associated hexachords, in other words, can not have more than this number of components in common, whatever the respective transpositional levels of the two set-forms.)

EXAMPLE 165

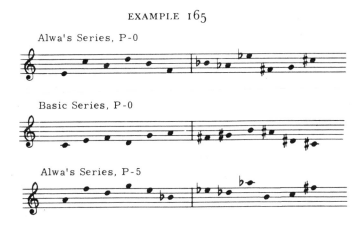

Although the inversional aspect of Dr. Schoen's series is clearly subordinate to the prime aspect, it is, curiously, this aspect rather than the prime that is associated with the principal referential forms of the basic series and Alwa's series, as well as with those of other, nonserial, sets. In example 166, I-0 of Dr. Schoen's series is seen to have maximum invariance with P-0 of the basic series (five common elements in corresponding hexachords).

EXAMPLE 166

The same form of Dr. Schoen's series completely duplicates the hexachordal content of the chief referential form, P-0, of Alwa's series (ex. 167):

EXAMPLE 167

Thus, although both Dr. Schoen's series and Alwa's series are noncombinatorial in the Schoenbergian sense—that is, hexachordal invariance cannot be established between a P- and I-form of the same series—they may be said to be "semi-combinatorial" in relation to each other, with segmental invariance occurring, however, between corresponding rather than noncorresponding hexachords. The pair of set-forms given in example 167 also preserves trichordal invariance (ex. 168), a relationship between the two sets that is exploited in Act III, Scene 2:

EXAMPLE 168

This total duplication of both hexachordal and trichordal content between I-0 of Dr. Schoen's series and P-0 of Alwa's series—a degree of association between independent series that is unique in the work—is evidently intended to symbolize their father-son relationship.

Example 95 illustrated another division of I-0 of Dr. Schoen's series, into a first segment of five and a second of seven notes. This segmentation of I-0 associates Dr. Schoen's series with a basic cell of the opera at the principal transpositional level of that cell (ex. 169, *a*). The same cell at another referential level, subordinate only to P-0, is embedded in the P-0 form of Dr. Schoen's series (ex. 169, *b*):

EXAMPLE 169

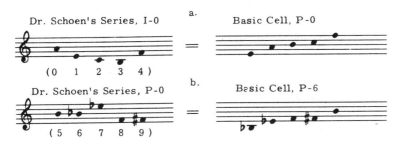

Via the basic cell, I-0 of Dr. Schoen's series is associated with Countess Geschwitz' trope (ex. 170, *a*).   Countess Geschwitz' trope is also related through its segmental structure to the Athlete's trope (ex. 170).

EXAMPLE 170

The chain of associations described above ultimately establishes a "family" of set-forms related through their similar partitioning of the semitonal scale (exx. 164, 165, 166, 167, 169, *a*, and 170). A hierarchy of tonal, or rather "twelve-tonal," harmonic areas is thus generated without the rigorous procedures of combinatoriality that have been described earlier, though the principles of set-structure upon which both depend are the same. Neither "combinatorially" nor "associatively" is there a strict compositional alignment of set-forms. The restriction of set-complexes to prime, or, at the most, prime and inversional forms, and the characterization of each series through a typical contour, limits the ambiguities that might otherwise arise, so that, with the establishment of clearly referential pitch levels and the frequently explicit presentation of sets as segmental structures, the differentiation of harmonic areas is effective even in sections of the work that do not explicitly articulate the set-segments.

The principal form of Dr. Schoen's series, P-0, is not a member of the above-mentioned family of set-forms, in that it is maximally invariant not with P-0 and I-0 of the basic series, but with P-9 and I-9. The latter set-forms are maximally invariant with Dr. Schoen's series in its I-3 form as well, but on the basis of non-corresponding rather than corresponding hexachords (ex. 171):

EXAMPLE 171

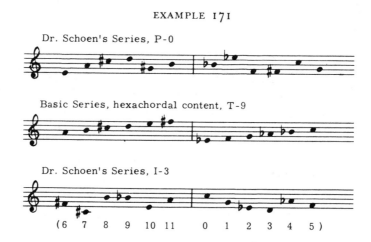

An illustration of the compositional exploitation of these relationships in the Prologue is given in examples 172-173. P-9 of the basic series is stated for the first time in bars 13-15 (violin and oboe). It last two notes are reiterated as the uppermost line of the Athlete's trope (the latter confirming the "home key" as established in bars 9 ff.). I-9 commences with its second hexachord, so that the hexachordal content with which P-9 concluded is repeated in bars 16 f. After the return of that segment in bars 18 f., the five notes that it shares with the second segment of Dr. Schoen's series in P-0 are sustained in a vertical statement of the latter segment, against a linear statement of the first segment of P-0 of Dr. Schoen's series (the first representation of this set in the opera).

Overlapping statements of various forms of Dr. Schoen's series in bars 20-24 are illustrated in example 173.[21] These forms are restricted to those shown in

---

[21] The reader who is making use of the piano-vocal reduction rather than the orchestral score in connection with this discussion should correct the vocal part in bar 22, the third note of which should read *b*, rather than *a*.

EXAMPLE 172

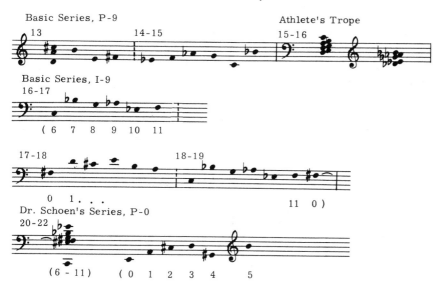

EXAMPLE 173

example 171, with the exception of a statement of the first hexachord of I-6, which occurs as an explicit motivic inversion (bars 22 f., viola and contrabass) of the first hexachord of P-0 as given in the cello, bars 20-21.

The associations of content that motivate the appearance of this segment of I-6 are shown in example 174. It is stated simultaneously with, and exactly duplicates the content of, order nos. 4 through 9 of P-0. Each of the associated hexachords comprises as well the same five-note collection, representing the above-mentioned basic cell at P-6, its secondary referential pitch level (cf. example 169, *b*). (The same cell at P-0 is given to the voice in bar 19.)

EXAMPLE 174

The only other statement of Dr. Schoen's series in the Prologue occurs at bars 64-65. The choice of set-forms, P-9, is determined by the return, in the preceding bar, of the basic series in P-0. The linear association of the two set-forms is based on maximum invariance (five common elements) between the adjacently stated hexachords (ex. 175).

EXAMPLE 175

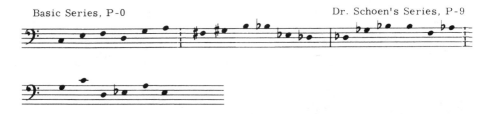

The characterization of each series by referential contours provides another basis for set association, premised on ordered rather than unordered invariance. In this respect too the basic series has priority over all other sets. Melodic cells embedded in the first hexachord of the basic series and their duplication in other serial sets are illustrated in example 176.

EXAMPLE 176

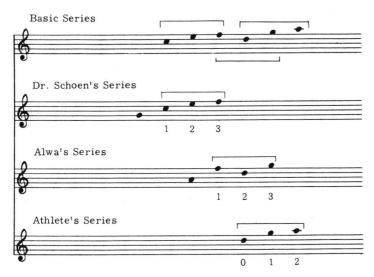

Such linear identities provide not only a basis for the association of different series, but also possible ambiguities that may be compositionally exploited. The rise of the curtain on the first scene of Act I introduces such an ambiguity (ex. 177). The first four notes of Alwa's series are heard, with the first note sustained in the orchestra and the following three sung by Alwa. The set that is actually unfolding, however, is the basic series, with its first two notes given to the orchestra and Alwa continuing with a segment that corresponds in order

EXAMPLE 177

Berg, Lulu, Act I, Sc. 1.

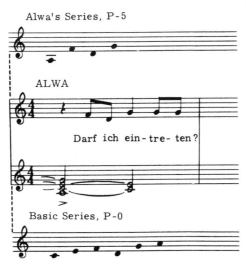

and typical contour to a segment of his own series. Although ordered invariance has not, in this work at least, the large structural implications of unordered invariance, its importance in establishing incidental and immediate associations among the various sets is comparable.

The structural functions of the tropes illustrated in example 178 derive from a segmental property which uniquely characterizes them among the many sets employed in the opera. Each of their component segments may not only be inverted, but also transposed without revision of pitch content. The all-combinatorial tetrachords on which they are based were given above, in source sets (2) and (1) of example 161, *a*. Although only a few complete set-statements of these tropes occur, they nevertheless have a salient position in the work due to their signal dramatic functions and distinctive musical character. The segment whose successive transpositions generate trope I—the set with which the opera opens—is the principal basic cell of the work. The limited number of nonequivalent set-forms generated by each of these tropes (two by trope I, one by trope II, three by trope III) renders them unsuitable for general compositional purposes but all the more fitting for the special roles assigned to them in the musical and dramatic design.

EXAMPLE 178

Schigolch's serial trope (ex. 107) is derived from the tetrachordally segmented semitonal scale (source set (3) of example 161, *a*). In terms of unordered segmental content, the set-complex generated by Schigolch's serial trope comprises only four nonequivalent pitch levels. In identifying Lulu's "father" with a trope whose tetrachordal content is that of the semitonal scale, Berg represents not only Lulu's shadowy background but also that of the opera itself, for it is only the semitonal scale, not the basic series, that one may justly describe as the ultimate source of all its cells and sets.[22]

Berg's preservation of contour is the diametric opposite of Webern's preservation of fixed octave positions, for the latter impose different contours on

---

[22]See Perle, "The Music of *Lulu*: A New Analysis," *Journal of the American Musicological*

different set-forms. It is possible that without this unique feature of Berg's twelve-tone idiom a number of the other distinctive features of that idiom would not be tenable. However, the significance of Berg's preservation of identical registral relationships among independent series, as in example 109, so that the referential contour of one series is embedded, so to speak, in that of another, remains unclear, apart from the relatively unimportant exception of a few passages where such a relationship between series is explicitly demonstrated. An impressive instance occurs at the moment of Dr. Schoen's death (Act II, bars 591-602), where his series is absorbed into the basic series (ex. 179).

EXAMPLE 179

The referential contours of other serial sets may be similarly related to that of the basic series, even where no explicit compositional statement of such a relationship is offered.

Many of the compositional procedures described in the course of this study are only ambiguously related, or even inconsistent with, the supposed assumptions of Schoenberg's "method of composing with twelve notes." I have tried to indicate the nature of the musical problems and purposes that underlie these ambiguities and revisions. The distinctive features of Berg's twelve-tone practice are not to be explained away, as they have been, as "licenses," motivated by a romantic indifference to the "rules" of "strict" twelve-tone composition, for the coherence of Berg's twelve-tone music depends on exactly the same properties of set-structure as the twelve-tone music of Schoenberg and Webern. The concepts of segmentation and inversional complementation ultimately permit a generalized description of twelve-tone pitch relations, the implications of which are not encompassed by these "rules."[23] The common ground shared by these and other composers of our time is of more interest and significance than the fact that compositional procedures are available that are entirely consistent with the postulates of Schoenberg's twelve-tone system.

Society, XII (1959), 195 f. This article should not be read without reference to my later study, "*Lulu*: Thematic Material and Pitch Organization," *Music Review*, XXVI (1965), 269 ff. The above discussion revises some details in the latter article as well.

   [23]This generalized description and its implications are the subject of my second book, *Twelve-Tone Tonality* (University of California Press, 1977).

Appendix

The nonequivalent pitch-class collections tabulated in section VIII of Chapter V are given below in pitch-class number notation. Each collection is given as an unordered segment of a bisected twelve-tone set. Pitch-class numbers will be based on 12 as the sum of each pair of inversionally complementary pitch-class numbers where an even number is assumed for that sum, and 11 where an odd number is assumed.[1] Thus all inversional relations will be represented by one or the other of the following series of dyads:

$$
\begin{array}{ccccccc}
0 & 1 & 2 & 3 & 4 & 5 & 6 \\
12 & 11 & 10 & 9 & 8 & 7 & 6
\end{array}
$$

$$
\begin{array}{cccccc}
0 & 1 & 2 & 3 & 4 & 5 \\
11 & 10 & 9 & 8 & 7 & 6
\end{array}
$$

Every symmetrical (that is, self-invertible) collection is shown in terms of these dyadic relations. For example, the fact that the "diminished-seventh chord" (four-note collection no. 1) is such a collection, and may therefore be inverted without revision of its content, is indicated by the vertical alignment of its mutually complementary pitch-class numbers. But in the case of this collection, other inversional relations exist which will maintain the same set of pitch-class numbers. These are shown by the T numbers, each of which may be applied as an alternative sum of complementary pitch-class numbers without revision of the collection:

$$
\begin{array}{ccc|cc|ccc|cc}
0 & 3 & 6 & 0 & 6 & 0 & 3 & 9 & 0 & 3 \\
\underline{12} & \underline{9} & \underline{6} & \underline{3} & \underline{9} & \underline{6} & \underline{3} & \underline{9} & \underline{9} & \underline{6} \\
12 & 12 & 12 & 3 & 15(=3) & 6 & 6 & 18(=6) & 9 & 9
\end{array}
$$

---

[1]The inversionally complementary relations of all sets are those given in the vertical intervals generated by the simultaneous statement of two chromatic scales proceeding in opposite directions. The cycle of vertical intervals will be either 0, 2, 4, 6, 8, 10, 12, or 1, 3, 5, 7, 9, 11, depending on whether the sum of complementary pitch-class numbers is even or odd. Since transposition is not a factor in the above presentation, a single even number and a single odd number may be assumed throughout as the respective sums of complementary pitch-class numbers (cf. p. 3).

The T numbers also show that the given collection is self-transposable, that is, it can be restated without revision of pitch-class content at each level represented by the given T numbers. All of these properties are equally characteristic of the eight-note segment of the same set. The symbol (g4) immediately to the left of the "diminished-seventh chord" applies only to the initial segment and indicates that successive transpositions of that collection by T–4 will generate a twelve-tone source set. The same result will follow when the generating interval is revised through the addition of any one of the T numbers that stand between the two segments. Thus, in this instance, the generating intervals are 4, 7, 10, and 1 (or the difference between any one of these and 12). Each collection that is not self-invertible is vertically aligned with a complementary "p" or "i" collection.

Six-note collections nos. 1 through 6, and 27p and i, are given only in the left column, since the twelve-tone set in each of these instances is completed by transposition of the given collection. Six-note collections that are designated by the same number but differentiated by the letters "A" and "B" are segments of the same twelve-tone set, but they are not equivalent as pitch-class collections, since neither by transposition, nor by inversion, nor by these operations combined, can the pitch-class content of either segment be transformed into that of the other segment.[2]

The hexachordal sets numbered 14 through 26 are the source sets of the Schoenbergian type of semi-combinatorial series. In the case of these sets only, I have aligned mutually complementary pitch-class collections horizontally rather than vertically. Hexachordal sets numbered 1 through 6 are the all-combinatorial source sets; 7 through 13 the P/RI semi-combinatorial source sets; 27 the P/P-T semi-combinatorial source sets.[3] Hexachordal sets num-

---

[2]They are, however, intervallically equivalent, in the sense that the collection of interval numbers comprised within the unordered pitch-class collection is the same for the one segment as for the other, just as, more obviously, it is for segments that are related by inversion or transposition. For example, the intervallic content of any one of the four hexachords numbered 28 is as follows:

Interval no.:	1(11)	2(10)	3(9)	4(8)	5(7)	6
Number of occurrences:	4	3	3	2	2	1

There is no correspondence, however, in the way these intervals are distributed in the respective A and B hexachords. Thus, the two occurrences of interval no. 5(7) in Ap represent the relations of three pitch-class numbers (2-7-0), while the two occurrences of the same interval in Bp represent two independent dyads (5-10, 6-11). (The two occurrences of this interval in each of the respective i hexachords are derived, of course, from the complements of these pitch-class numbers.) Pitch-class collections are discussed in terms of their intervallic content by David Lewin, in "Intervallic Relations Between Two Collections of Notes," *The Journal of Music Theory*, III (1959) 298 ff. and "The Intervallic Content of a Collection of Notes," *ibid.*, IV (1960) 98 ff., and by Allen Forte in *The Structure of Atonal Music* (New Haven: Yale University Press, 1973).

[3]These and segmental collections derived from other partitionings of the source sets are discussed in terms of their combinatorial implications by Donald Martino, "The Source Set and Its Aggregate Formations," *The Journal of Music Theory*, V (1961), 224 ff. Combinatoriality as based on any set and any segmentation is discussed in Daniel Starr and Robert Morris, "A General Theory of Combinatoriality and the Aggregate," *Perspectives of New Music*, XVI/1 (1977), 3ff. and XVI/2 (1978), 50ff.

bered 28 through 35 are, in a conventional sense, noncombinatorial. Combinatorial relations can be asserted, however, between *different* series based on the same "noncombinatorial" source set (cf. p. 138, above).

Pitch-class collections are most conveniently identified by a series of interval numbers showing the differences between successive (in increasing order) pitch-class numbers. The advantage of naming pitch-class collections in this way is that the same series of integers (in one or another circular permutation) will express the relations of a series of pitch classes, regardless of the numbers assigned to the latter. For illustration, let us take four-note collection no. 4, represented in the following table by successive pitch-class numbers 0 2 9 11 (0). Subtracting each integer from the one to its right, we derive the interval series 2 7 2 1. The same collection may also be represented by successive pitch-class numbers 0 7 9 10 (0), or 0 2 3 5 (0), or 0 1 3 10 (0), since each of these collections is equivalent to the first by permutation and transposition. This equivalence is made immediately evident when we substitute the respective interval-number series: 7 2 1 2, 2 1 2 7, 1 2 7 2.[4]

RELATIVE PITCH-CLASS COLLECTIONS

No.	One-Note Collection					No.	Eleven-Note Collection					
1. (g1,g5)	0 / 12					1.	1 / 11	2 / 10	3 / 9	4 / 8	5 / 7	6 / 6

No.	Two-Note Collections						No.	Ten-Note Collections					
1. (g1,g5)	3 / 9						T-6 1.	0 / 12	1 / 11	2 / 10	4 / 8	5 / 7	6 / 6
2. (g2)	0 / 11						2.	1 / 10	2 / 9	3 / 8	4 / 7	5 / 6	
3. (g2)	1 / 10						3.	0 / 11	2 / 9	3 / 8	4 / 7	5 / 6	
4. (g2)	2 / 9						4.	0 / 11	1 / 10	3 / 8	4 / 7	5 / 6	
5.	1 / 11						5.	0 / 12	2 / 10	3 / 9	4 / 8	5 / 7	6 / 6
6.	2 / 10						6.	0 / 12	1 / 11	3 / 9	4 / 8	5 / 7	6 / 6

---

[4]This method of naming pitch-class collections was proposed by Eric Regener in his article, "On Allen Forte's Theory of Chords," *Perspectives of New Music*, XIII/I (1974), pp. 195 f., and by Richard A. Chrisman in his dissertation (Yale University, 1969), *A Theory of Axis-Tonality for Twentieth-Century Music*.

No.	Three-Note Collections		
1. (g3)	0 4 / 12 8	T-4, T-8	
2. (g3)	0 1 / 12 11		
3. (g3)	0 2 / 12 10		
4. (g3)	0 5 / 12 7		
5.	0 3 / 12 9		
6p. (g3)	0 1 5		
6i. (g3)	11 10 6		
7p.	0 1 3		
7i.	11 10 8		
8p.	0 1 4		
8i.	11 10 7		
9p.	0 1 6		
9i.	11 10 5		
10p.	0 2 5		
10i.	11 9 6		
11p.	0 2 6		
11i.	11 9 5		
12p.	0 4 9		
12i.	11 7 2		

No.	Nine-Note Collections
1.	1 2 3 5 6 / 11 10 9 7 6
2.	2 3 4 5 6 / 10 9 8 7 6
3.	1 3 4 5 6 / 11 9 8 7 6
4.	1 2 3 4 6 / 11 10 9 8 6
5.	1 2 4 5 6 / 11 10 8 7 6
6p.	2 3 4 6 7 8 9 10 11
6i.	9 8 7 5 4 3 2 1 0
7p.	2 4 5 6 7 8 9 10 11
7i.	9 7 6 5 4 3 2 1 0
8p.	2 3 5 6 7 8 9 10 11
8i.	9 8 6 5 4 3 2 1 0
9p.	2 3 4 5 7 8 9 10 11
9i.	9 8 7 6 4 3 2 1 0
10p.	1 3 4 6 7 8 9 10 11
10i.	10 8 7 5 4 3 2 1 0
11p.	1 3 4 5 7 8 9 10 11
11i.	10 8 7 6 4 3 2 1 0
12p.	1 2 3 5 6 7 8 10 11
12i.	10 9 8 6 5 4 3 1 0

No.	Four-Note Collections	
1. (g4)	0 3 6 / 12 9 6	T-3, T-6, T-9
2. (g4)	0 5 / 11 6	T-6
3. (g4)	0 1 / 11 10	

No.	Eight-Note Collections
1.	1 2 4 5 / 11 10 8 7
2.	1 2 3 4 / 10 9 8 7
3.	2 3 4 5 / 9 8 7 6

No.	Four-Note Collections	No.	Eight-Note Collections
4. (g4)	0 2 / 11 9	4.	1 3 4 5 / 10 8 7 6
5. (g4)	1 3 / 10 8	5.	0 2 4 5 / 11 9 7 6
6. (g4)	0 5 6 / 12 7 6	6.	1 2 3 4 / 11 10 9 8
7.	2 4 / 10 8	T-6 7.	0 1 3 5 6 / 12 11 9 7 6
8.	1 2 / 11 10	8.	0 3 4 5 6 / 12 9 8 7 6
9.	1 2 / 10 9	9.	0 3 4 5 / 11 8 7 6
10.	2 3 / 10 9	10.	0 1 4 5 6 / 12 11 8 7 6
11.	1 3 / 11 9	11.	0 2 4 5 6 / 12 10 8 7 6
12.	0 3 / 11 8	12.	1 2 4 5 / 10 9 7 6
13.	1 4 / 11 8	13.	0 2 3 5 6 / 12 10 9 7 6
14.	0 4 / 11 7	14.	1 2 3 5 / 10 9 8 6
15.	0 4 6 / 12 8 6	15.	1 2 3 5 / 11 10 9 7
16p. (g4)	0 1 3 6	16p.	2 4 5 7 8 9 10 11
16i. (g4)	11 10 8 5	16i.	9 7 6 4 3 2 1 0
17p.	0 1 2 4	17p.	3 5 6 7 8 9 10 11
17i.	11 10 9 7	17i.	8 6 5 4 3 2 1 0
18p.	0 1 2 5	18p.	3 4 6 7 8 9 10 11
18i.	11 10 9 6	18i.	8 7 5 4 3 2 1 0
19p.	0 1 2 6	19p.	3 4 5 7 8 9 10 11
19i.	11 10 9 5	19i.	8 7 6 4 3 2 1 0
20p.	0 1 3 5	20p.	2 4 6 7 8 9 10 11
20i.	11 10 8 6	20i.	9 7 5 4 3 2 1 0

No.	Four-Note Collections	No.	Eight-Note Collections
21p.	0 1 3 7	21p.	2 4 5 6 8 9 10 11
21i.	11 10 8 4	21i.	9 7 6 5 3 2 1 0
22p.	0 1 3 8	22p.	2 4 5 6 7 9 10 11
22i.	11 10 8 3	22i.	9 7 6 5 4 2 1 0
23p.	0 1 3 9	23p.	2 4 5 6 7 8 10 11
23i.	11 10 8 2	23i.	9 7 6 5 4 3 1 0
24p.	0 1 4 6	24p.	2 3 5 7 8 9 10 11
24i.	11 10 7 5	24i.	9 8 6 4 3 2 1 0
25p.	0 1 4 7	25p.	2 3 5 6 8 9 10 11
25i.	11 10 7 4	25i.	9 8 6 5 3 2 1 0
26p.	0 1 4 8	26p.	2 3 5 6 7 9 10 11
26i.	11 10 7 3	26i.	9 8 6 5 4 2 1 0
27p.	0 1 5 7	27p.	2 3 4 6 8 9 10 11
27i.	11 10 6 4	27i.	9 8 7 5 3 2 1 0
28p.	0 2 4 7	28p.	1 3 5 6 8 9 10 11
28i.	11 9 7 4	28i.	10 8 6 5 3 2 1 0
29p.	0 2 5 8	29p.	1 3 4 6 7 9 10 11
29i.	11 9 6 3	29i.	10 8 7 5 4 2 1 0

	Five-Note Collections		Seven-Note Collections
1.	0 1 2 12 11 10	1.	3 4 5 6 9 8 7 6
2.	0 2 3 12 10 9	2.	1 4 5 6 11 8 7 6
3.	0 3 4 12 9 8	3.	1 2 5 6 11 10 7 6
4.	0 4 5 12 8 7	4.	1 2 3 6 11 10 9 6
5.	0 1 3 12 11 9	5.	2 4 5 6 10 8 7 6
6.	0 2 4 12 10 8	6.	1 3 5 6 11 9 7 6
7.	0 3 5 12 9 7	7.	1 2 4 6 11 10 8 6

No.	Five-Note Collections					No.	Seven-Note Collections						
8.	0	1	4			8.	2	3	5	6			
	12	11	8				10	9	7	6			
9.	0	2	5			9.	1	3	4	6			
	12	10	7				11	9	8	6			
10.	0	1	5			10.	2	3	4	6			
	12	11	7				10	9	8	6			
11p.	0	1	2	3	5	11p.	4	6	7	8	9	10	11
11i.	11	10	9	8	6	11i.	7	5	4	3	2	1	0
12p.	0	1	2	3	6	12p.	4	5	7	8	9	10	11
12i.	11	10	9	8	5	12i.	7	6	4	3	2	1	0
13p.	0	1	2	3	7	13p.	4	5	6	8	9	10	11
13i.	11	10	9	8	4	13i.	7	6	5	3	2	1	0
14p.	0	1	2	4	5	14p.	3	6	7	8	9	10	11
14i.	11	10	9	7	6	14i.	8	5	4	3	2	1	0
15p.	0	1	2	4	6	15p.	3	5	7	8	9	10	11
15i.	11	10	9	7	5	15i.	8	6	4	3	2	1	0
16p.	0	1	2	4	7	16p.	3	5	6	8	9	10	11
16i.	11	10	9	7	4	16i.	8	6	5	3	2	1	0
17p.	0	1	2	4	8	17p.	3	5	6	7	9	10	11
17i.	11	10	9	7	3	17i.	8	6	5	4	2	1	0
18p.	0	1	2	4	9	18p.	3	5	6	7	8	10	11
18i.	11	10	9	7	2	18i.	8	6	5	4	3	1	0
19p.	0	1	2	5	6	19p.	3	4	7	8	9	10	11
19i.	11	10	9	6	5	19i.	8	7	4	3	2	1	0
20p.	0	1	2	5	7	20p.	3	4	6	8	9	10	11
20i.	11	10	9	6	4	20i.	8	7	5	3	2	1	0
21p.	0	1	2	5	8	21p.	3	4	6	7	9	10	11
21i.	11	10	9	6	3	21i.	8	7	5	4	2	1	0
22p.	0	1	2	6	7	22p.	3	4	5	8	9	10	11
22i.	11	10	9	5	4	22i.	8	7	6	3	2	1	0
23p.	0	1	3	4	6	23p.	2	5	7	8	9	10	11
23i.	11	10	8	7	5	23i.	9	6	4	3	2	1	0
24p.	0	1	3	4	7	24p.	2	5	6	8	9	10	11
24i.	11	10	8	7	4	24i.	9	6	5	3	2	1	0

No.	Five-Note Collections					No.	Eight-Note Collections						
25p.	0	1	3	5	7	25p.	2	4	6	8	9	10	11
25i.	11	10	8	6	4	25i.	9	7	5	3	2	1	0
26p.	0	1	3	5	8	26p.	2	4	6	7	9	10	11
26i.	11	10	8	6	3	26i.	9	7	5	4	2	1	0
27p.	0	1	3	5	9	27p.	2	4	6	7	8	10	11
27i.	11	10	8	6	2	27i.	9	7	5	4	3	1	0
28p.	0	1	3	5	10	28p.	2	4	6	7	8	9	11
28i.	11	10	8	6	1	28i.	9	7	5	4	3	2	0
29p.	0	1	3	6	7	29p.	2	4	5	8	9	10	11
29i.	11	10	8	5	4	29i.	9	7	6	3	2	1	0
30p.	0	1	3	6	8	30p.	2	4	5	7	9	10	11
30i.	11	10	8	5	3	30i.	9	7	6	4	2	1	0
31p.	0	1	3	6	9	31p.	2	4	5	7	8	10	11
31i.	11	10	8	5	2	31i.	9	7	6	4	3	1	0
32p.	0	1	3	6	10	32p.	2	4	5	7	8	9	11
32i.	11	10	8	5	1	32i.	9	7	6	4	3	2	0
33p.	0	1	3	7	8	33p.	2	4	5	6	9	10	11
33i.	11	10	8	4	3	33i.	9	7	6	5	2	1	0
34p.	0	1	3	7	9	34p.	2	4	5	6	8	10	11
34i.	11	10	8	4	2	34i.	9	7	6	5	3	1	0
35p.	0	1	3	8	9	35p.	2	4	5	6	7	10	11
35i.	11	10	8	3	2	35i.	9	7	6	5	4	1	0
36p.	0	1	4	5	8	36p.	2	3	6	7	9	10	11
36i.	11	10	7	6	3	36i.	9	8	5	4	2	1	0
37p.	0	1	4	6	8	37p.	2	3	5	7	9	10	11
37i.	11	10	7	5	3	37i.	9	8	6	4	2	1	0
38p.	0	1	4	6	9	38p.	2	3	5	7	8	10	11
38i.	11	10	7	5	2	38i.	9	8	6	4	3	1	0

Six-Note Collections   Six-Note Collections

1. (g1,g5) $\begin{matrix} 0 & 2 & 4 & 6 \\ 12 & 10 & 8 & 6 \end{matrix}$ T-2, T-4, T-6, T-8, T-10

2. (g2) $\begin{matrix} 0 & 3 & 4 \\ 11 & 8 & 7 \end{matrix}$ T-4, T-8

No.	Six-Note Collections		No.	Six-Note Collections
3. (g3)	0 1 5 6 12 11 7 6	T-6		
4. (g6)	0 1 2 11 10 9			
5. (g6)	0 1 3 11 10 8			
6. (g6)	0 2 4 11 9 7			
7A.	0 4 5 6 12 8 7 6		7B.	1 2 3 11 10 9
8A.	0 4 5 11 7 6		8B.	1 2 3 10 9 8
9A.	0 2 3 11 9 8		9B.	1 4 5 10 7 6
10A.	0 2 5 6 12 10 7 6		10B.	1 3 4 11 9 8
11A.	0 2 5 11 9 6		11B.	1 3 4 10 8 7
12A.	0 1 3 6 12 11 9 6		12B.	2 4 5 10 8 7
13A.	0 2 3 6 12 10 9 6		13B.	1 4 5 11 8 7
14p.	0 1 3 6 7 9 T-6		14i.	11 10 8 5 4 2
15p.	0 1 2 3 4 6		15i.	11 10 9 8 7 5
16p.	0 1 2 3 5 7		16i.	11 10 9 8 6 4
17p.	0 1 2 3 6 7		17i.	11 10 9 8 5 4
18p.	0 1 2 4 5 8		18i.	11 10 9 7 6 3
19p.	0 1 2 4 6 8		19i.	11 10 9 7 5 3
20p.	0 4 6 8 9 10		20i.	11 7 5 3 2 1
21p.	0 4 5 8 9 10		21i.	11 7 6 3 2 1
22p.	0 1 2 5 7 8		22i.	11 10 9 6 4 3

No.	Six-Note Collections						No.	Six-Note Collections					
23p.	0	1	3	4	6	9	23i.	11	10	8	7	5	2
24p.	0	3	5	7	9	10	24i.	11	8	6	4	2	1
25p.	0	1	4	6	8	9	25i.	11	10	7	5	3	2
26p.	0	1	3	5	7	9	26i.	11	10	8	6	4	2
27p. (g6)	0	1	2	4	5	9							
27i. (g6)	12	11	10	8	7	3							
28Ap.	0	1	2	3	4	7	28Bp.	5	6	8	9	10	11
28Ai.	11	10	9	8	7	4	28Bi.	6	5	3	2	1	0
29Ap.	0	1	2	3	5	8	29Bp.	4	6	7	9	10	11
29Ai.	11	10	9	8	6	3	29Bi.	7	5	4	2	1	0
30Ap.	0	1	2	3	5	9	30Bp.	4	6	7	8	10	11
30Ai.	11	10	9	8	6	2	30Bi.	7	5	4	3	1	0
31Ap.	0	1	2	3	6	8	31Bp	4	5	7	9	10	11
31Ai.	11	10	9	8	5	3	31Bi.	7	6	4	2	1	0
32Ap.	0	1	2	4	6	9	32Bp.	3	5	7	8	10	11
32Ai.	11	10	9	7	5	2	32Bi.	8	6	4	3	1	0
33Ap.	0	1	2	4	7	8	33Bp.	3	5	6	9	10	11
33Ai.	11	10	9	7	4	3	33Bi.	8	6	5	2	1	0
34Ap.	0	1	2	4	7	9	34Bp.	3	5	6	8	10	11
34Ai.	11	10	9	7	4	2	34Bi.	8	6	5	3	1	0
35Ap.	0	1	2	5	6	9	35Bp.	3	4	7	8	10	11
35Ai.	11	10	9	6	5	2	35Bi.	8	7	4	3	1	0

INTERVAL-NUMBER SERIES

No.	One-Note Collection		No.	Eleven-note Collection										
1. (g1,g5)	0		1	1	1	1	1	1	1	1	1	1	1	2

No.	Two-Note Collections			No.	Ten-Note Collections									
1. (g1,g5)	6	6	T-6 1.		1	1	2	1	1	1	1	2	1	1
2. (g2)	11	1		2.	1	1	1	1	1	1	1	1	1	3
3. (g2)	9	3		3.	2	1	1	1	1	1	1	1	2	1
4. (g2)	7	5		4.	1	2	1	1	1	1	1	2	1	1

Two-Note Collections

5.	10	2
6.	8	4

Three-Note Collections

1. (g3)	4	4	4	T-4, T-8
2. (g3)	1	10	1	
3. (g3)	2	8	2	
4. (g3)	5	2	5	
5.	3	6	3	
6p. (g3)	1	4	7	
6i. (g3)	7	4	1	
7p.	1	2	9	
7i.	9	2	1	
8p.	1	3	8	
8i.	8	3	1	
9p.	1	5	6	
9i.	6	5	1	
10p.	2	3	7	
10i.	7	3	2	
11p.	2	4	6	
11i.	6	4	2	
12p.	4	5	3	
12i.	3	5	4	

Four-Note Collections

1. (g4)	3	3	3	3	T-3, T-6, T-9
2. (g4)	5	1	5	1	T-6
3. (g4)	1	9	1	1	
4. (g4)	2	7	2	1	
5. (g4)	2	5	2	3	
6. (g4)	5	1	1	5	

Ten-Note Collections

5.	2	1	1	1	1	1	1	1	1	2
6.	1	2	1	1	1	1	1	1	2	1

Nine-Note Collections

1.	1	1	2	1	1	2	1	1	2
2.	1	1	1	1	1	1	1	1	4
3.	2	1	1	1	1	1	1	2	2
4.	1	1	1	2	2	1	1	1	2
5.	1	2	1	1	1	1	2	1	2
6p.	1	1	2	1	1	1	1	1	3
6i.	3	1	1	1	1	1	2	1	1
7p.	2	1	1	1	1	1	1	1	3
7i.	3	1	1	1	1	1	1	1	2
8p.	1	2	1	1	1	1	1	1	3
8i.	3	1	1	1	1	1	1	2	1
9p.	1	1	1	2	1	1	1	1	3
9i.	3	1	1	1	1	2	1	1	1
10p.	2	1	2	1	1	1	1	1	2
10i.	2	1	1	1	1	1	2	1	2
11p.	2	1	1	2	1	1	1	1	2
11i.	2	1	1	1	1	2	1	1	2
12p.	1	1	2	1	1	1	2	1	2
12i.	2	1	2	1	1	1	2	1	1

Eight-Note Collections

1.	1	2	1	2	1	2	1	2
2.	1	1	1	3	1	1	1	3
3.	1	1	1	1	1	1	1	5
4.	2	1	1	1	1	1	2	3
5.	2	2	1	1	1	2	2	1
6.	1	1	1	4	1	1	1	2

Four-Note Collections

7.	2	4	2	4
8.	1	8	1	2
9.	1	7	1	3
10.	1	6	1	4
11.	2	6	2	2
12.	3	5	3	1
13.	3	4	3	2
14.	4	3	4	1
15.	4	2	2	4
16p. (g4)	1	2	3	6
16i. (g4)	6	3	2	1
17p.	1	1	2	8
17i.	8	2	1	1
18p.	1	1	3	7
18i.	7	3	1	1
19p.	1	1	4	6
19i.	6	4	1	1
20p.	1	2	2	7
20i.	7	2	2	1
21p.	1	2	4	5
21i.	5	4	2	1
22p.	1	2	5	4
22i.	4	5	2	1
23p.	1	2	6	3
23i.	3	6	2	1
24p.	1	3	2	6
24i.	6	2	3	1
25p.	1	3	3	5
25i.	5	3	3	1
26p.	1	3	4	4
26i.	4	4	3	1

Eight-Note Collections

T-6 7.	1	2	2	1	1	2	2	1
8.	3	1	1	1	1	1	1	3
9.	3	1	1	1	1	1	3	1
10.	1	3	1	1	1	1	3	1
11.	2	2	1	1	1	1	2	2
12.	1	2	1	1	1	2	1	3
13.	2	1	2	1	1	2	1	2
14.	1	1	2	1	2	1	1	3
15.	1	1	2	2	2	1	1	2
16p.	2	1	2	1	1	1	1	3
16i.	3	1	1	1	1	2	1	2
17p.	2	1	1	1	1	1	1	4
17i.	4	1	1	1	1	1	1	2
18p.	1	2	1	1	1	1	1	4
18i.	4	1	1	1	1	1	2	1
19p.	1	1	2	1	1	1	1	4
19i.	4	1	1	1	1	2	1	1
20p.	2	2	1	1	1	1	1	3
20i.	3	1	1	1	1	1	2	2
21p.	2	1	1	2	1	1	1	3
21i.	3	1	1	1	2	1	1	2
22p.	2	1	1	1	2	1	1	3
22i.	3	1	1	2	1	1	1	2
23p.	2	1	1	1	1	2	1	3
23i.	3	1	2	1	1	1	1	2
24p.	1	2	2	1	1	1	1	3
24i.	3	1	1	1	1	2	2	1
25p.	1	2	1	2	1	1	1	3
25i.	3	1	1	1	2	1	2	1
26p.	1	2	1	1	2	1	1	3
26i.	3	1	1	2	1	1	2	1

Four-Note Collections

27p.	1	4	2	5
27i.	5	2	4	1
28p.	2	2	3	5
28i.	5	3	2	2
29p.	2	3	3	4
29i.	4	3	3	2

Eight-Note Collections

27p.	1	1	2	2	1	1	1	3
27i.	3	1	1	1	2	2	1	1
28p.	2	2	1	2	1	1	1	2
28i.	2	1	1	1	2	1	2	2
29p.	2	1	2	1	2	1	1	2
29i.	2	1	1	2	1	2	1	2

Five-Note Collections

1.	1	1	8	1	1
2.	2	1	6	1	2
3.	3	1	4	1	3
4.	4	1	2	1	4
5.	1	2	6	2	1
6.	2	2	4	2	2
7.	3	2	2	2	3
8.	1	3	4	3	1
9.	2	3	2	3	2
10.	1	4	2	4	1
11p.	1	1	1	2	7
11i.	7	2	1	1	1
12p.	1	1	1	3	6
12i.	6	3	1	1	1
13p.	1	1	1	4	5
13i.	5	4	1	1	1
14p.	1	1	2	1	7
14i.	7	1	2	1	1
15p.	1	1	2	2	6
15i.	6	2	2	1	1
16p.	1	1	2	3	5
16i.	5	3	2	1	1
17p.	1	1	2	4	4
17i.	4	4	2	1	1

Seven-Note Collections

1.	1	1	1	1	1	1	6
2.	3	1	1	1	1	3	2
3.	1	3	1	1	3	1	2
4.	1	1	3	3	1	1	2
5.	2	1	1	1	1	2	4
6.	2	2	1	1	2	2	2
7.	1	2	2	2	2	1	2
8.	1	2	1	1	2	1	4
9.	2	1	2	2	1	2	2
10.	1	1	2	2	1	1	4
11p.	2	1	1	1	1	1	5
11i.	5	1	1	1	1	1	2
12p.	1	2	1	1	1	1	5
12i.	5	1	1	1	1	2	1
13p.	1	1	2	1	1	1	5
13i.	5	1	1	1	2	1	1
14p.	3	1	1	1	1	1	4
14i.	4	1	1	1	1	1	3
15p.	2	2	1	1	1	1	4
15i.	4	1	1	1	1	2	2
16p.	2	1	2	1	1	1	4
16i.	4	1	1	1	2	1	2
17p.	2	1	1	2	1	1	4
17i.	4	1	1	2	1	1	2

Five-Note Collections						Seven-Note Collections							
18p.	1	1	2	5	3	18p.	2	1	1	1	2	1	4
18i.	3	5	2	1	1	18i.	4	1	2	1	1	1	2
19p.	1	1	3	1	6	19p.	1	3	1	1	1	1	4
19i.	6	1	3	1	1	19i.	4	1	1	1	1	3	1
20p.	1	1	3	2	5	20p.	1	2	2	1	1	1	4
20i.	5	2	3	1	1	20i.	4	1	1	1	2	2	1
21p.	1	1	3	3	4	21p.	1	2	1	2	1	1	4
21i.	4	3	3	1	1	21i.	4	1	1	2	1	1	4
22p.	1	1	4	1	5	22p.	1	1	3	1	1	1	4
22i.	5	1	4	1	1	22i.	4	1	1	1	3	1	1
23p.	1	2	1	2	6	23p.	3	2	1	1	1	1	3
23i.	6	2	1	2	1	23i.	3	1	1	1	1	2	3
24p.	1	2	1	3	5	24p.	3	1	2	1	1	1	3
24i.	5	3	1	2	1	24i.	3	1	1	1	2	1	3
25p.	1	2	2	2	5	25p.	2	2	2	1	1	1	3
25i.	5	2	2	2	1	25i.	3	1	1	1	2	2	2
26p.	1	2	2	3	4	26p.	2	2	1	2	1	1	3
26i.	4	3	2	2	1	26i.	3	1	1	2	1	2	2
27p.	1	2	2	4	3	27p.	2	2	1	1	2	1	3
27i.	3	4	2	2	1	27i.	3	1	2	1	1	2	2
28p.	1	2	2	5	2	28p.	2	2	1	1	1	2	3
28i.	2	5	2	2	1	28i.	3	2	1	1	1	2	2
29p.	1	2	3	1	5	29p.	2	1	3	1	1	1	3
29i.	5	1	3	2	1	29i.	3	1	1	1	3	1	2
30p.	1	2	3	2	4	30p.	2	1	2	2	1	1	3
30i.	4	2	3	2	1	30i.	3	1	1	2	2	1	2
31p.	1	2	3	3	3	31p.	2	1	2	1	2	1	3
31i.	3	3	3	2	1	31i.	3	1	2	1	2	1	2
32p.	1	2	3	4	2	32p.	2	1	2	1	1	2	3
32i.	2	4	3	2	1	32i.	3	2	1	1	2	1	2
33p.	1	2	4	1	4	33p.	2	1	1	3	1	1	3
33i.	4	1	4	2	1	33i.	3	1	1	3	1	1	2
34p.	1	2	4	2	3	34p.	2	1	1	2	2	1	3
34i.	3	2	4	2	1	34i.	3	1	2	2	1	1	2

Five-Note Collections

35p.	1	2	5	1	3
35i.	3	1	5	2	1
36p.	1	3	1	3	4
36i.	4	3	1	3	1
37p.	1	3	2	2	4
37i.	4	2	2	3	1
38p.	1	3	2	3	3
38i.	3	3	2	3	1

Seven-Note Collections

35p.	2	1	1	1	3	1	3
35i.	3	1	3	1	1	1	2
36p.	1	3	1	2	1	1	3
36i.	3	1	1	2	1	3	1
37p.	1	2	2	2	1	1	3
37i.	3	1	1	2	2	2	1
38p.	1	2	2	1	2	1	3
38i.	3	1	2	1	2	2	1

Six-Note Collections

1. (g1,g5)	2	2	2	2	2	2
2. (g2)	3	1	3	1	3	1
3. (g3)	1	4	1	1	4	1
4. (g6)	1	1	7	1	1	1
5. (g6)	1	2	5	2	1	1
6. (g6)	2	2	3	2	2	1

Six-Note Collections

T–2, T–4, T–6, T–8, T–10

T–4, T–8

T–6

7A.	4	1	1	1	1	4	7B.	1	1	6	1	1	2
8A.	4	1	1	1	4	1	8B.	1	1	5	1	1	3
9A.	2	1	5	1	2	1	9B.	3	1	1	1	3	3
10A.	2	3	1	1	3	2	10B.	2	1	4	1	2	2
11A.	2	3	1	3	2	1	11B.	2	1	3	1	2	3
12A.	1	2	3	3	2	1	12B.	2	1	2	1	2	4
13A.	2	1	3	3	1	2	13B.	3	1	2	1	3	2
14p.	1	2	3	1	2	3	T–6 14i.	3	2	1	3	2	1
15p.	1	1	1	1	2	6	15i.	6	2	1	1	1	1
16p.	1	1	1	2	2	5	16i.	5	2	2	1	1	1
17p.	1	1	1	2	2	5	17i.	5	2	2	1	1	1
18p.	1	1	2	1	3	4	18i.	4	3	1	2	1	1
19p.	1	1	2	2	2	4	19i.	4	2	2	2	1	1

Six-Note Collections							Six-Note Collections					
20p.	4	2	2	1	1	2	20i.	2	1	1	2	2	4
21p.	4	1	3	1	1	2	21i.	2	1	1	3	1	4
22p.	1	1	3	2	1	4	22i.	4	1	2	3	1	1
23p.	1	2	1	2	3	3	23i.	3	3	2	1	2	1
24p.	3	2	2	2	1	2	24i.	2	1	2	2	2	3
25p.	1	3	2	2	1	3	25i.	3	1	2	2	3	1
26p.	1	2	2	2	2	3	26i.	1	3	2	2	1	3
27p. (g6)	1	1	2	1	4	3						
27i. (g6)	3	4	1	2	1	1						
28Ap.	1	1	1	1	3	5	28Bp.	1	2	1	1	1	6
28Ai.	5	3	1	1	1	1	28Bi.	6	1	1	1	2	1
29Ap.	1	1	1	2	3	4	29Bp.	2	1	2	1	1	5
29Ai.	4	3	2	1	1	1	29Bi.	5	1	1	2	1	2
30Ap.	1	1	1	2	4	3	30Bp.	2	1	1	2	1	5
30Ai.	3	4	2	1	1	1	30Bi.	5	1	2	1	1	2
31Ap.	1	1	1	3	2	4	31Bp.	1	2	2	1	1	5
31Ai.	4	2	3	1	1	1	31Bi.	5	1	1	2	2	1
32Ap.	1	1	2	2	3	3	32Bp.	2	2	1	2	1	4
32Ai.	3	3	2	2	1	1	32Bi.	4	1	2	1	2	2
33Ap.	1	1	2	3	1	4	33Bp.	2	1	3	1	1	4
33Ai.	4	1	3	2	1	1	33Bi.	4	1	1	3	1	2
34Ap.	1	1	2	3	2	3	34Bp.	2	1	2	2	1	4
34Ai.	3	2	3	2	1	1	34Bi.	4	1	2	2	1	2
35Ap.	1	1	3	1	3	3	35Bp.	1	3	1	2	1	4
35Ai.	3	3	1	3	1	1	35Bi.	4	1	2	1	3	1

Index

TO BASIC DEFINITIONS

Index
TO COMPOSITIONS

(Figures in boldface refer to examples; others to pages.)